Critical Conditions: My Diary of the Syrian Revolution

Hadi Abdullah
Translated by Alessandro Columbu

Critical Conditions: My Diary of the Syrian Revolution

Hadi Abdullah
Translated by **Alessandro Columbu**

DoppelHouse Press | Los Angeles
doppelhouse.com

Critical Conditions: My Diary of the Syrian Revolution

Hadi Abdullah
***Translated by* Alessandro Columbu**

Edited by Michael Beard
© 2025 DoppelHouse Press, Los Angeles
English translation and Introduction © 2025 Alessandro Columbu

Editor's Note © 2025 Michael Beard
Parts One, Two and Three © 2025 Hadi Abdullah

All photographs courtesy Hadi Abdullah, except pages 120, 269–271, and 274, where noted, which were sourced by the publisher from Hadi Abdullah's Facebook pages and videos, from the Radio Fresh Facebook and Ra'ed al-Fares's Facebook as well as other linked Facebook pages. The publisher has made best efforts to find the unknown photographers, and requests that anyone with further information come forward so that credits can be updated in future editions.

Book Design: Kourosh Biegpour | Typesetting: Carrie Paterson

Publisher's Cataloging-in-Publication Data

Names: Abdullah, Hadi, author. | Columbu, Alessandro, translator.
Title: Critical conditions : my diary of the Syrian revolution / by Hadi Abdullah; translated by Alessandro Columbu.
Description: Los Angeles, CA: DoppelHouse Press, 2025.
Identifiers: ISBN: 9781954600355 (hardcover) | 9781954600949 (paperback) | 9781954600362 (ebook)
Subjects: LCSH Abdullah, Hadi. | Syria--History--Civil War, 2011--- Personal narratives, Syrian. | Syria--History--Civil War, 2011---Biography. | Revolutions--Syria--History--21st century. | War correspondents-- Syria--Biography. | BISAC BIOGRAPHY & AUTOBIOGRAPHY / Personal Memoirs | BIOGRAPHY & AUTOBIOGRAPHY / Arab & Middle Eastern | BIOGRAPHY & AUTOBIOGRAPHY / Editors, Journalists, Publishers
Classification: LCC DS98.6 .A33 2025 | DDC 956.9104/23--dc23

DoppelHouse Press | Los Angeles
doppelhouse.com

Contents

Introduction by the Translator

The old world is dying and the new world struggles to be born:
now is the time of monsters —Antonio Gramsci[1]

I'll start from the end, from that morning in December 2024 when I woke up to the images that we had been dreaming about for over thirteen years. The caption on the TV screen read: 'The Assad Regime Has Fallen'. I was crying, why? I couldn't believe it, and neither could my Syrian friends, and I still to this day haven't been able to process the enormity of the events. For over a decade, we had breathed this revolution, mourned its victims, witnessed its distortions, and endured its abandonment by the world. The morning the Assad regime fell though, time folded in on itself.

It is precisely in this context that the present book gains even greater relevance, not only as a chronicle of resistance but as a record of what led Syrians to risk everything for a different future. *Critical Conditions: My Diary of the Syrian Revolution* is a first-person account of the uprising starting in 2011 through the fall of the Assad regime on 8 December 2024, by Hadi Abdullah, a Syrian activist and independent reporter from al-Qusayr, near Homs. His memoirs capture sentiments and choices that are crucial to remember as the country begins to reckon with its past and imagine what might come next. His short, impressionistic chapters capture the daily reality of the Revolution through a mix of personal narrative and field reporting. The protagonists are an entire generation of Syrians who responded to repression and violence with a sense of purpose, courage, and collective resolve in the face of widespread oppression and arbitrariness from the regime, its allies in Iran, Lebanon and Russia, as well as extremist groups such as ISIS and Jabhat al-Nusra.

I was a twenty-five-year-old Arabic literature and language student just returning from Damascus when the Syrian Revolution erupted in March 2011. Reading Hadi's memoir for the first time, when it came out in Arabic back in 2020, brought back so many memories of those days in 2011 and 2012, when the news of mass demonstrations coming from Syria made change and freedom seem possible. Every Friday, activists called for a new demonstration on their social media pages: the Friday of Rage, the Friday of Dignity, the Friday of 'Leave!', the Friday of the Free Syrian Army. Soon demonstrations were taking place regularly in most Syrian provinces, but Fridays were particularly popular because more people could easily get time off work. With these demonstrations, an endless list of slogans and catchphrases became popularised in Syria and abroad, among the Syrian diaspora and anyone who was curious about the then promising developments in this country with whom so many of us had fallen in love: 'You're next, doctor' said one slogan (which rhymes in Arabic, *Ajāk addūr yā duktūr* – اجاك الدور يا دكتور), the 'doctor' being Bashar al-Assad himself in a subtle mockery of the Syrian regime propaganda, which would occasionally refer to its leader as 'adduktūr', the doctor, because of Assad's brief spell as an ophthalmology student in London in the 1990s. The broader meaning can be understood in the context of the Arab Spring, which in 2011 had witnessed other long-lasting Arab dictators such as Ben Ali, Mubarak and

Gaddafi succumb to weeks and weeks of protests, sit-ins, demonstrations and clashes with the police. Assad was next then, and according to this slogan it was only a matter of time before his entourage turned their back on him and allowed for change to take place. Other slogans were more easily intelligible but required a background in the regime's own decades-old slogans, which so many Syrians had been accustomed to reciting in school or at orchestrated demonstrations. 'God… Syria… freedom, that's it!' (Allāh, Sūriyya, ḥurriyyah wa bas! – الله، سوريا، حرّية وبس) mirrored the regime's equivalent, in which the word freedom was replaced with Bashar. Same goes for 'We sacrifice our blood and our souls for your sake oh martyr!' (Bi'r-rūḥ, bi'd-dam, nafdīk yā shahīd – بالروح، بالدم نفديك يا شهيد). In the regime's equivalent, the word martyr had been replaced with… Bashar again, or sometimes his father's name, Hafiz.

Following the events of the Revolution and passionately witnessing the developments on the ground also involved learning about prominent figures on the regime side, some of whom are mentioned in this book, even if only in passing. One of the slogans cited by Hadi for example goes, Yā 'Ātif, yā Najīb, bidnā ninassīk al-ḥalīb – يا عاطف يا نجيب بدنا ننسيك الحليب, which literally translates as 'Atef Najib we will make you forget milk', but since it rhymes in Arabic and is understood as a threat, I rendered it as 'Atef Najib we'll make you regret you left your crib'. A cousin of Bashar al-Assad, Najib is considered to have contributed significantly to the outbreak of protests. In March 2011, a group of boys in Daraa were arrested for writing anti-government slogans such as 'You're next, doctor' on their school walls. Atef Najib, as head of the security services in Daraa at the time, was accused of ordering the brutal arrest and severe mistreatment of those boys, sparking widespread protests among residents demanding their release. When the government refused and responded by shooting live ammunition at the protestors, the state of unrest escalated. Daraa became a focal point for nationwide demonstrations against the Assad regime. Atef Najib's harsh response to the initial protests in Daraa is often seen as a catalyst for the wider anti-government movement across Syria because of his heavy-handed methods, including the use of violence.

Especially the first eighty pages of this memoir reveal the perception that ordinary Syrians like Hadi had of their government and its security services before 2011. A sense of terror permeated the conversations surrounding the regime and its official corps, particularly the most feared *mukhabarat*, i.e. intelligence services, and the unofficial thugs known as *shabbihah*. Emerging in the late 1970s, the shabbihah were primarily involved in smuggling and extortion, but they gradually gained more power, operating with impunity and behaving similarly to mafia-style organisations, with protection from and collaboration with Syrian state authorities. Over time, the shabbihah became known for extreme brutality, exploiting their close ties to the regime and terrorising communities through violence, looting, and rape. The regime used them as a reflection of its core survival strategy – relying on thuggish enforcers to maintain control and suppress dissent.

As it emerges from Hadi's experience, they certainly lived up to their infamous reputation after 2011 as an essential and indispensable element in the regime's policy of counterinsurgency that targeted peaceful civilians and armed protestors almost indiscriminately. And yet, despite the oppressive presence of the shabbihah and the brutal repression by the Assad regime, these memoirs illuminate the enduring power of memory and the resilience of truth. Hadi Abdullah's accounts serve as a potent reminder that even in the face of overwhelming violence and state-sponsored terror, the act of bearing witness through storytelling can be a powerful form of resistance. This is further amplified by the crucial role played by numerous local Syrian and transnational Arab TV networks, which have provided a platform for these narratives to reach a wider audience, and which proved essential to spread Hadi's independent reporting. As Hadi's memoirs show, particularly in the first fifteen chapters, media outlets such as Sham and Orient, though often operating under immense pressure, became indispensable in preserving the historical record and ensuring that the voices of those who suffered under the regime were not silenced.

Given the evocative nature of Hadi's writing, rich in metaphor and symbolic resonance, several recurring terms in the memoir deserve closer attention. One of the most prominent is the word *martyr* (Arabic: *shahīd* – شهيد), which Hadi uses not only to describe civilians killed in the regime's indiscriminate bombings, but more often to honour the unsung heroes of the Syrian Revolution, who died too young, murdered by the Syrian regime for daring to protest, organise and document what was happening. For Hadi then, the term carries both emotional and political weight, transforming individual loss into a symbol of collective resistance and sacrifice. In this sense, through the pages of these memoirs the reality of civil society and grassroots movements that originated in Syria, perhaps for the first time since its independence, emerges in all its power. The centrality of the concept of friendship also transpires as having acted as the binding force between men who had been complete strangers to each other until marches, protests and a thirst for change brought them together.

Among the many symbolic elements and metaphors, few images in this memoir are as emotionally charged and resonant as the jasmine flower. Often associated with Damascus, jasmine came to represent the peaceful origins of the revolution, as well as love, memory, and the enduring spirit of hope. Also known as the Damascus jasmine (Jasminum Damascenum), jasmine has long been intertwined with Syrian culture, heritage, and everyday life. Damascus, often referred to as the City of Jasmine, is known for its streets filled with the scent. During the early days of the Syrian revolution, activists adopted jasmine as a symbol of non-violent resistance and peaceful protest. In a context where demonstrations were initially peaceful, the jasmine flower embodied the hope for a peaceful transition to a more just and democratic society. The stories of activists reflect this yearning, describing how the flower was used to convey messages of hope, unity, and resilience in the face of oppression. As the Revolution evolved into a more violent conflict, jasmine came to symbolise a stark contrast to the brutality of the Assad regime's crackdown. On more than one occasion in this book, jasmine is evoked as a reminder of the purity of their intentions and the original spirit of the Revolution, a movement that sought freedom and dignity and rejected violence. In Hadi's memoirs, jasmine also takes on a role as a symbol of love and purity, sometimes as the 'seed of the Revolution which take a long time to grow branches and climb walls', other times to symbolise the soothing effect elicited by his beloved wife, Rafah.

Equally poetic is Hadi's use of the Arabic word *'ayn* (عين), literally meaning 'eye', as an expression of deep affection and camaraderie when referring to his close friends. By doing so, he poetically emphasises the significance and cherished status they hold in his life, equating their value metaphorically to the preciousness of one's eyesight. It's common in Arabic to address someone dear as *yā 'aynī* (يا عيني, 'O my eye') or even use the plural *'uyūnī* (عيوني, 'my eyes') – expressions that imply the person is as cherished as one's vision, essentially the 'apple of one's eye'. Common idioms like *nūr 'aynī* (نور عيني, 'light of my eye') in love songs exemplify this usage, suggesting the loved one illuminates the speaker's life. Consequently, readers encounter chapters titled or prominently featuring the word eye/eyes, reflecting Hadi's emotional bond and heartfelt appreciation for the friendships he treasures.

I feel the English reader will benefit from a brief introduction to Syria's geography and the location of the main cities and areas mentioned throughout these memoirs. Originally from al-Qusayr, a small town near the border with Lebanon, Hadi attended the first demonstrations in the city of Homs, sometimes referred to as 'the capital of the Syrian revolution'. Located in central-western Syria, between the border with Lebanon and the coastal mountains to the west and the Syrian Desert to the east, Homs lies on a plateau along the banks of the Orontes River, approximately 160 kilometres north of Damascus. Most of the first part of the book takes place in this area, with Hadi and his friends gravitating in and around Homs to report on the demonstrations and the armed conflict that ensued, until June 2013 when the local residents were expelled (the events of this painful uprooting are told in the chapter 'Exiting Paradise'). In hindsight, the summer of 2013 was indeed a watershed moment for the Syrian Revolution, but one could argue for the entire Arab Spring. In the space of a few weeks between June and August, with the indispensable aid of its Hezbollah allies, the Syrian regime reconquered entire cities and areas which had previously been liberated by the opposition, and on 21 August, the infamous chemical attack (known in Syria as al-Kimāwī) in the Damascus suburb of al-Ghoutah claimed the lives of hundreds of innocent civilians who died from suffocation, having inhaled chlorine gas. Earlier in July, in nearby Egypt, the short-lived rule of the first democratically elected government in the country's history was brought to an end by a military coup d'état led by Field Marshall Abdelfattah el-Sisi, which inaugurated a period of restauration of the former regime of military authoritarianism.

Seeking refuge, Hadi and his friends made their way to the Qalamoun region, a rugged and mountainous area in southwestern Syria that stretches along the Anti-Lebanon mountain range. Located northeast of Damascus and bordering Lebanon, Qalamoun occupies a strategic position along the highway connecting Damascus to Homs. Its steep terrain and proximity to the Lebanese border made it a haven for those displaced by violence, as well as a key area in the broader conflict due to its control over vital supply routes. For Hadi, it offered a temporary shelter amidst the chaos, a place to regroup and plan his next move.

Later, Hadi's journey took him to Kafranbel, a small town nestled in the southern part of the Idlib Governorate, roughly 35 kilometres south of Idlib in the Northwest of Syria. Though unassuming in size and located in a largely rural area dominated by rolling hills and fertile plains, Kafranbel rose to international prominence during the Syrian conflict. The town became a symbol of the Syrian uprising, not through military actions or strategic importance, but through the creativity and courage of its residents. Ra'ed al-Fares and other activists from Kafranbel gained global recognition for their use of satirical banners and slogans that communicated the plight of ordinary Syrians to the world. Written in both Arabic and English, these messages were crafted to resonate with an international audience, highlighting the brutality of the regime and the suffering caused by war while also addressing the indifference or inaction of global powers. What made Kafranbel stand out was the combination of wit and artistry in its slogans. These banners, held up during demonstrations or posted online, did more than just demand freedom or denounce oppression, they often cleverly critiqued global politics, called out hypocrisy, and appealed directly to the humanity of viewers. The town's residents, armed with little more than markers and poster boards, managed to achieve what many larger movements struggled to do: connect the personal and political, giving a voice to the voiceless in a way that was impossible to ignore.

For Hadi, arriving in Kafranbel meant entering a place where resistance was an act of creativity and defiance. Here, amidst the challenges of war, the town's spirit served as a reminder that even the smallest of places could leave an indelible mark on the world. Kafranbel, though battered by violence and loss, remained a beacon of resilience, its banners echoing far beyond its borders.

In 2016, Hadi's journey brought him to Aleppo, Syria's second largest city located in the northwestern part of the country near the border with Türkiye. By this time, Aleppo, once Syria's thriving economic and cultural hub, was one of the fiercest battlegrounds of the Syrian conflict, the city being under intense siege by regime forces. The battle for Aleppo had escalated into a devastating campaign that divided the city between the government-held west and rebel-held east. The eastern neighborhoods, where Hadi found himself, were encircled by regime forces, cutting off vital supply lines and subjecting the area to relentless aerial bombardments. Life in the besieged areas was marked by unimaginable hardship, with civilians and fighters alike enduring severe shortages of food, medical supplies, and basic necessities. By December 2016, the siege reached its climax. After months of escalating assaults and dwindling resources, the rebel forces in eastern Aleppo faced inevitable defeat. The regime's final push, aided by allied militias and Russian air support, overwhelmed the remaining defences. Under a deal brokered to end the fighting, tens of thousands of civilians and rebels were evacuated from the city. The exodus marked a bitter chapter in the war. For Hadi, leaving Aleppo was not just an act of survival but also a moment of profound loss marked by the critical injury of his friend and cameraman, Khaled al-'Issa.

In this part of his memoir, it becomes evident how the protest movement was increasingly undermined by the rise of extremist factions such as Jabhat al-Nusra (of which the newly appointed Syrian president, Ahmed Hussein al-Sharaa, was a prominent member and military leader) and ISIS (the so-called Islamic State). These groups brought with them a rigid ideological framework and a disregard for the civic values that had defined the early Revolution and therefore diverged sharply from that of the original grassroots activists. As these factions gained ground, militarily and politically, they imposed repressive rule in areas that had been liberated by activists and local councils, often eradicating the very movements that had first challenged the regime. Their presence gave the Assad government a pretext to frame the entire uprising as a terrorist insurgency. This shift further alienated international allies, complicated aid and media coverage, and devastated the networks of civilian resistance that had taken years to build. For many

Syrians, these groups represented another source of violence as well as a betrayal of the Revolution's original ideals: freedom, dignity, and non-sectarian political change.

Hadi Abdullah speaks directly to this tension in his memoir. After relocating to northern Syria, particularly in areas around Idlib and Kafranbel, he recounts his direct confrontations with Jabhat al-Nusra. Unlike many who chose silence or exile, Hadi continued to speak out publicly against the group's abuses, including its harassment of activists, suppression of dissent, and attempts to monopolise media and narrative control. His refusal to remain silent came at great personal risk and stresses the complexity of the Syrian battlefield, where opposition to Assad did not always mean shared values or goals. Hadi's stance illustrates the persistence of revolutionary ethics in the face of new forms of authoritarianism and shows that the fight for justice extended beyond the regime to any group that sought to undermine the principles of the uprising.

Anyone curious about Syria in the past fifteen years will find Hadi Abdullah's memoirs to be a compelling testimony of Syria's youth ardour and struggle for justice that has no equivalent. Hadi's account of his activism and his passion for the cause of the Syrian revolution is enriched by the sentimental dimension of his writing, the detailed description of his inner feelings, his emotions and his anxieties; by recounting his and his friends' feelings of hope, joy, liberation as well as vulnerability, dispossession and defeat; by his personal experience of emancipation and the heavy price he has paid to achieve that: the separation from his family, the death of his four best friends (and fellow media activists), the multiple attempts on his life at the hands of the Syrian regime and its allies. What makes his account so compelling is how deeply he digs into the emotional experience of being part of this pivotal moment in history. Through his words, you can sense the intensity of hope, fear, uncertainty, and determination that permeated the air. You feel the weight of the moment, the kind of weight that leaves an imprint on one's soul, long after the events have passed. Incredibly, the text itself became even more poignant as the Assad regime collapsed during the time it took me to translate it. This transformation from current reporting to a historical record highlights its significance, not just as a chronicle of events, but an intensely personal testament of a moment that will be etched into history.

In December 2024, Syria entered a new phase of political transformation after more than a decade of civil war and sixty years of authoritarian rule. Though the future remains uncertain, this moment marked the end of an era defined by repression, war, and displacement. Hadi speaks to the new reality in Part Three, which I translated from dozens of WhatsApp voice memos as he and I corresponded this spring. In translating this memoir, I tried to preserve both the content and the feeling. What makes Hadi's story so powerful is not just what he saw, but how he experienced it – the hope, the fear of irreversible decisions. That emotional truth is what gives this book its lasting force, and what I hope English readers can now share. As Syria enters a future full of unknowns, Hadi's testimony reminds us why so many chose to rise up in the first place. In the spirit of Antonio Gramsci, whose words have long guided those resisting oppression: *'I'm a pessimist because of intelligence, but an optimist because of will'.* That tension, between the reality of what was and the hope for what could be, runs through every page of this memoir.

Alessandro Columbu
London, May 2025

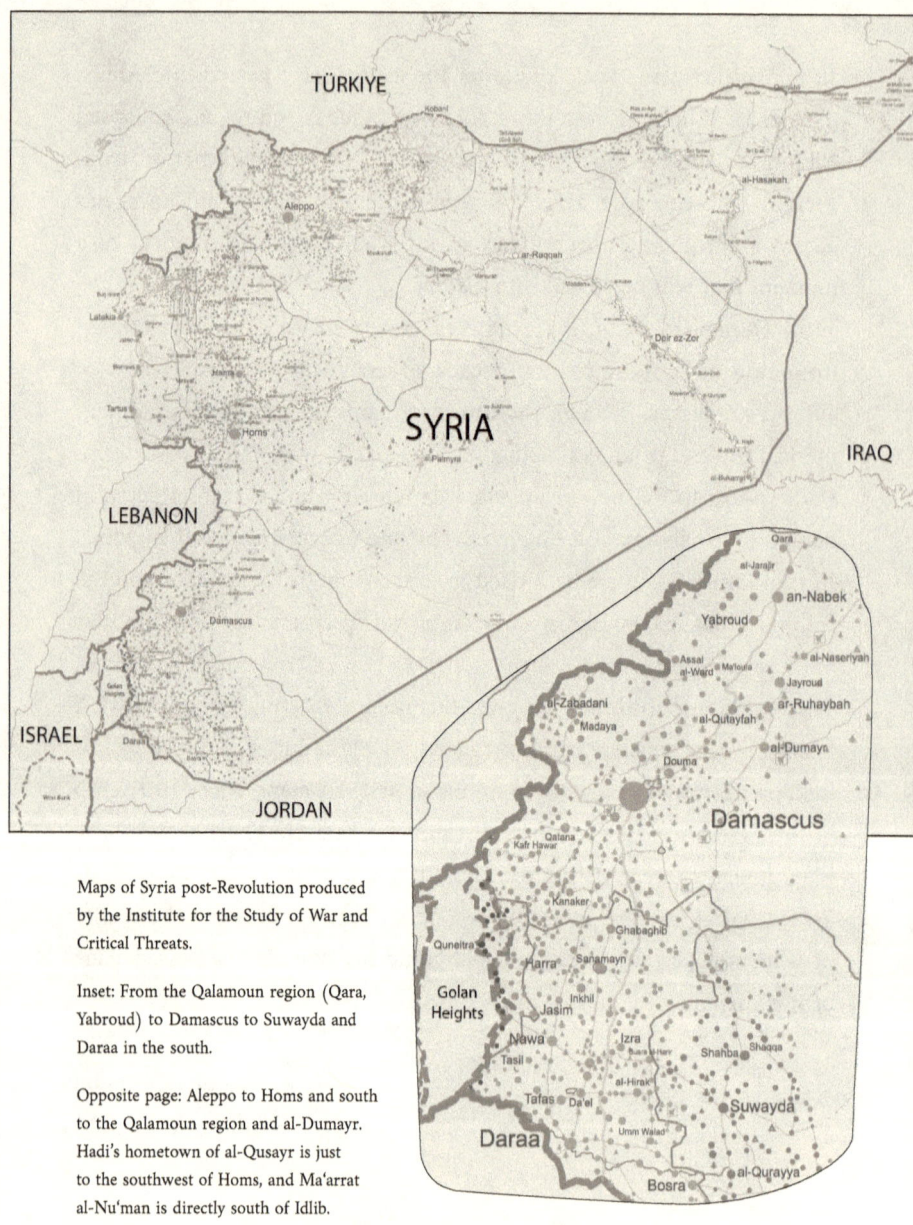

Maps of Syria post-Revolution produced by the Institute for the Study of War and Critical Threats.

Inset: From the Qalamoun region (Qara, Yabroud) to Damascus to Suwayda and Daraa in the south.

Opposite page: Aleppo to Homs and south to the Qalamoun region and al-Dumayr. Hadi's hometown of al-Qusayr is just to the southwest of Homs, and Ma'arrat al-Nu'man is directly south of Idlib.

In this book, Maarrat al-Nu'man is spelled Ma'arrat al-Nu'man and Kafr Nabl (just west of Ma'arrat al-Nu'man) has been transliterated as Kafranbel. For readability and accuracy in a book, colored areas showing control by different factions have been removed from the original map dated 9 May 2025. Creative Commons Attribution 4.0 International.

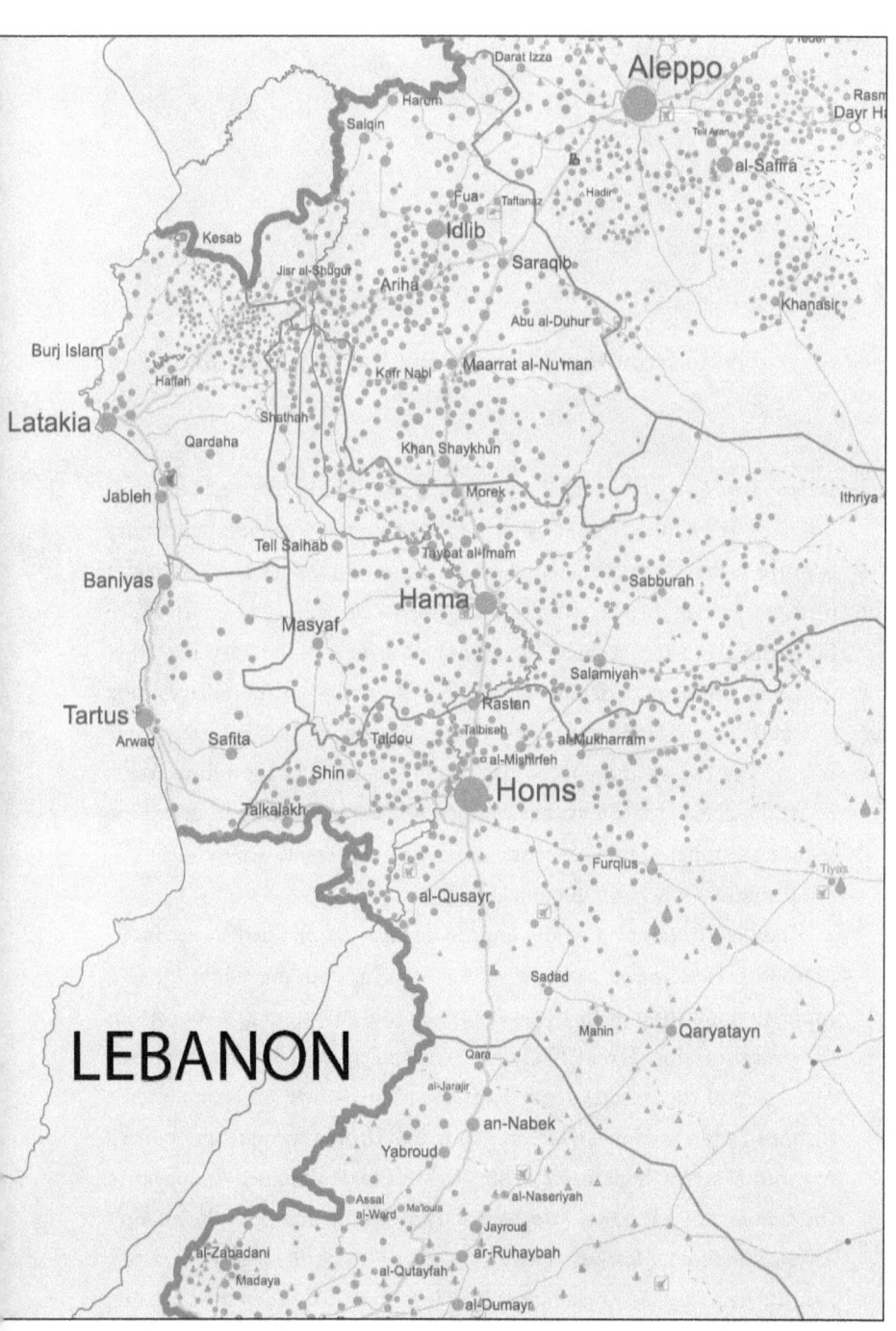

Note from the Editor of the English Edition

What particularly characterises Hadi Abdullah's *Critical Conditions* is its intimacy. It's a history of resistance to an oppressive power, but history seen from the inside. Official works of history look back from a greater distance, identifying big trends and patterns of cause and effect which bind one event to another. The author of a personal history has other goals. You meet his friends and family; you see what the villages look like and how it feels when they are threatened or attacked by regime forces. The causes and effects that matter stretch into the future. What holds the events together is aspirational: the determination to defeat the seemingly undefeatable government powers and create a new society. What matters is what will come next.

Abdullah does not give the impression that he planned to become a journalist. He lets you see how events, step by step, drew him into his profession, starting with the account of the government's monstrous over-reaction, in March 2011, to teenagers' graffiti in Daraa, on the other side of the country from his home of al-Qusayr, and soon after, a demonstration in Homs which began in the Droubi mosque and poured out into Martyrs' Square. He begins to send texts designed to appear in the captions of TV news. (He even shows you his first text: '*Homs: large demonstration on Martyrs' Square in solidarity with the people of Daraa. Security forces shot live ammunition leading to casualties and injuries*'.) Later, he phones in reports using a disguised voice to remain anonymous. He runs into the photojournalist Tarad al-Zuhouri (he can't remember how) and under his apprenticeship becomes a journalist himself, travelling to demonstrations and conflicts with his own crew of technicians and also uploading reports to social media.

Critical Conditions (*Ḥālāt ḥarijah*) shows us the story behind his broadcast reports, what happened between one and the next, how it felt to be there and what toll it took, emotionally and physically. Official histories of the future will be likely to analyse government pronouncements and the positions of revolutionaries. In this book you get an account of the chants devised for demonstrations, and the texts of ingenious graffiti, the cunning, often brilliant miniatures compressing insults, cries of rage, satire, and mockery into messages short enough to be inked onto cardboard or sheets, the smallest units of historical discourse. Official histories of those demonstrations and the armed conflicts will list the number of casualties. Here you mourn the death of friends. (You can learn more about one of them, Ra'ed al-Fares and Radio Fresh, on an episode of *This American Life*: 'Wartime Radio'.)

Critical Conditions, in its original Arabic edition as published in 2020, comprises the first two parts of this book. Alessandro Columbu finished this translation in June 2024. Six months later, in December, when Bashar al-Assad decamped and the government fell, it became clear how appropriate it would be to include the course of those interim four years in the story to create a narrative with historical symmetry. The result is Part Three, which owes its existence to WhatsApp. It was conveyed orally, transcribed and translated from voice memos, about ten minutes long (56 of them) recorded between March and May 2025.

The three parts blend seamlessly. The book as published in 2020 ended with a mission, on June of 2019, during disastrous air attacks on Idlib province from government and Russian forces. Hadi leaves from Maʿarrat al-Nuʿman where his media centre Radio Fresh was located, to rescue a group of friends hemmed in by Russian air fire and wounded by a land mine near Morek, about 20 miles away, to bring them back to safety after a Russian airstrike. This is where the book in Arabic ends, clearly aware that the story would continue. Part Three picks up the story the same day and takes us through the successes and set-backs which continue for the next five years of the conflict, the birth of his two children, and constant threats from outside, which include an earthquake as devastating as a rocket attack. It ends with the fall of the regime and two days later, his return to his childhood home in al-Qusayr. It's a kind of closure, but, again, the end of a memoir is never the end of the story.

There are historical settings which we remember by their architecture: mansard roofs in 18th-century France, tract houses in post-war America, skyscrapers in any contemporary big city, council housing in the periphery. Perhaps we're living in an age where the emblematic urban scene is rubble… the sight of a family's personal lives, their furniture, children's toys, clothes closets and cooking utensils all open to the passer-by, the walls without their verticality, now fragments with rebar poking out. Gaza. Sudan. Ukraine, Iran, Iraq, endless vistas of shattered glass and toppling masonry. It would be easier for us to ignore them if it were not for journalists willing to run towards the disaster. The televised report shows us the damage. This memoir goes further. It imagines what might happen, a world without fear where those cityscapes might be rebuilt. There are no guarantees that will happen, and official histories are neutral on the subject. This book gives us the persistent vision of hope.

Michael Beard
20 June 2025

Note from the Editor of the Arabic Edition

This book is my contribution to the Revolution, to Muhammad and Zaynah, and it's the least I can do.

Let me point out that what you are going to read is made of selections from a life story, told only by Hadi Abdullah himself. The book does not follow the structure of a novel, nor does it comply with the principles of documentation. This book does not tell everything about the Syrian Revolution, but it tells the story of its author through his memories. It doesn't exaggerate the importance of a certain battle or the role of some military division or the dignity of any martyr. The contents reflect the opinions of its author, his point of view and his experience as a journalist.

Important: *all passages in italics were transcribed exactly as told by the author,* everything else was written in accordance with the principles of storytelling.

Jude

9 August 2019

Reporting from the scene as people tear down a billboard with Bashar al-Assad. Instagram post.

Selfie request from a fan while people hoist new flags and banners. Instagram post.

Reporting from the Damascene Sword memorial after the liberation of Damascus. Instagram post.

Reporting from the aftermath of a bombing. Instagram post.

First live report showing his full face, but still using the pseudonym 'Hadi Abdullah'. Broadcast on al-Jazeera from al-Qusayr, 12 April 2012. Archived at https://m.youtube.com/watch?v=dHkR5umpuvE.

Reporting from the Martyr's Square clocktower in Homs after the fall of the Assad regime. Instagram post.

Interviewing children street vendors after the fall of the Assad regime. Instagram post.

Foreword

It was Jude who came up with the idea of writing my story. Against the vast expanse of events that weighed us down, confronted with the extent of injustice and hardship that my compatriots have to endure and the torment and sadness that floods over them after every new life lesson, Jude's suggestion was to tell my story from the beginning of the Revolution – recounting with my voice what I had captured with my camera plus those experiences which weren't in my social media or in the limited personal information you could find in my reports from the battlefield.

At first, I dismissed the idea, thinking it would be too difficult, if not impossible to accomplish. The events were just too complex. She said, we'll just set down some events that you still retain in your exhausted memory.

I said that a lot of people suffered more than I had, and had seen more suffering.

She said, consider your story like a younger sister to theirs. Everything deserves to be recorded. Consider it an attempt to rescue the facts from those who want to distort what happened and to remember the experiences of those whose voices might otherwise be gone forever.

The only solution was to write. And that's what we did.

Hadi

Part One 2011-2014

Prologue

At last, the young man graduated and found himself at a crossroads again. He knew what his next stage would be and had no fear for the future... It had been written for him before, and since he didn't have the qualifying marks to major in medicine, he specialised in nursing, specifically those cases in 'critical condition'. What happened, though, was impossible to foresee. His life became nothing more than a leaf on a tree in the thunderstorm of the war that broke out across the homeland. The moment the Revolution blossomed, he entered the operating room straightaway, to report the undistorted facts, except that from that time on, all conditions became critical.

Field reporting, with Ra'ed al-Fares as camerman.

Before the Beginning

They say life cannot be summarised in words. I disagree. I believe that words possess the capacity to express the realities of life, to convey its significance, its grievances, troubles and spells of restlessness at the simple strike of a pen. To record a whole story in the space of one line or two and, by doing so, salvage it from oblivion. When you speak, you don't want to miss anything. And yet you know that your confession won't capture every corner of your memory. There are things that we choose to forget and others that we keep buried so they don't expose our wounds, and yet others that we hope will just go away as if they never happened.

Where do I start? Or rather where does the story start? It would be okay if this were just one story. Sometimes life runs so smoothly it almost says to us, sum me up in a few words. Sometimes, though, life is so intense and eventful that, although we're about to finish our story, it seems to never end. Let me tell you this: there is one last ray of hope that I will come to at one point... perhaps that's what's kept me going to this day. And yet when I go to sleep, shortly before dawn, I recall everything that's happened, and I realise that the last few drops of water in a jar are those that can better quench one's thirst. I live now in constant fear of loss. I whisper things to God in the middle of the night as if I were delirious. Eternal separation has darkened my eyes twice. God, please don't let loss darken my heart.

You say, tell me the story in detail. I will tell it to you as long as my heart beats and my lungs breathe. But don't blame me if I don't finish the story. No matter what they promise to a country, wars are always a form of colonisation. I'm nothing more than a spectre staggering through my homeland under the bombing. As for the details, I'll tell you everything that hasn't escaped my mind, even after all the blows it has received.

It might sound strange to learn that I was a nurse before all this started. When you rewind the tape, you feel dumbfounded. How did all this happen, as if we were water running in a riverbed? We always strive to reach the sea, but do we realise how tiny we are? In our victories as in our defeats, in times of joy and in times of pain, with everything we have managed to take care of and with everything that slipped through our fingers, as water escapes our grip? In all the tragedies that we witness and experience? The sea is always more than you are and will be. It has a deep bottom and a faraway sky, and no way back. Like life itself.

Marks on the final exams in secondary school have always been the main obstacle between the personal ambitions of my fellow Syrians and reality. In popular anecdotes, the protagonists are usually either extraordinary geniuses or not very bright people. I, however, belong to neither of these two categories. I didn't have the necessary grades to enter the faculty of medicine, but my heart and mind were full of a desire to help others, and what's more noble than saving human lives? I gave this a considerable amount of thought and concluded that nursing was the best specialisation for me.

I didn't think too much about the future, but I had a feeling I was on the right path. I was heading to a place where I would be able to give, close to those who are suffering, offering them comfort and alleviating the pain of their wounds. In my mind, I had a clear vision of nursing as a heavenly message through which the most eminent signs of human compassion become manifest, but it had never crossed my mind that within a few years, my homeland would be devoid of the slightest of those signs.

As a student I excelled, for which I'm beholden to God. Thanks to my good grades I was able to go to Egypt to undertake further training during my third year. As I progressed in my studies and my graduation was approaching, I started contemplating the idea of doing postgraduate studies to specialise in critical care. I had hopes of becoming a teaching assistant and loved the idea of perhaps obtaining a PhD, something that would grant me the opportunity to deliver my message to the largest possible number of people. Training paramedics and nurses was the closest to being one of them that I was able to find. Day after day the dream was coming true until I was asked to teach at the faculty of nursing of al-Baath University in Hama.

At that time, the match of the Arab Revolutions was being lit, but we dismissed the idea that its flare could reach us. In secret conversations, we would discuss whether the examples of Egypt, Libya and Tunisia could be compared to Syria and its reality. When it was my turn to speak, I would fumble and hesitate between my desires and reality, between the sensible and the impossible. I was convinced that our national army in Syria would never side with the people against the regime and that therefore the price to pay would be high. Bringing down a dictatorship that had lasted for more than forty years would require walking down a long blood-stained carpet, and the dream of freedom would still remain far, far away.

Knocking on Freedom's Doors

17 February 2011

Some might say it happened unexpectedly, but jasmine seeds take a long time to grow branches and climb walls. The regime's oppression, coupled with the belief that *'walls have ears'* and can always hear everything, nurtured this growth. That is why its fragrance now fills the streets of Damascus.

'You're next, doctor! The people want to bring down the regime! Down with Bashar al-Assad!' This is what children wrote on the walls of the Arba'in School in Daraa, a city that had been suffocating under widespread oppression and corruption. Those children perhaps didn't know anything else besides those slogans that they probably heard on TV, but they saw them fit for the condition of an impoverished, tyrannized nation. Or perhaps they knew a lot more than that. Things deteriorated further when Atef Najib, Bashar al-Assad's maternal cousin, sent his men to arrest the children and scatter them between his jails and the air force intelligence offices in Damascus. When the sixteen children went missing for days and people found out that they had been tortured, their families went asking for them, but to no avail. The answer they received came as clear as the bitter reality people had had to tolerate and come to terms with: 'Forget your children. Go to your wives, knock them up and bear new children. If you can't do that because you're not men enough, let us know, our men would gladly impregnate them'.

Truth is, the Assad regime thinks of Syria as its little plantation, and of Syrians as slaves. That's what lit up a Revolution whose first martyrs were fifteen-year-old kids. The voice of slogans and chants started to rise. 'Death before humiliation!' alongside 'O, Atef – O, Najib, you'll regret you left your crib!'

The day the contagion spread to Damascus, and its people became infected with rage, we followed the events closely on TV as well as on the internet. The jasmine was the seed of the Revolution, and Damascus was its hotbed, naturally, as its people soon started echoing the chants of those in Daraa. People rose, led by the voice of 'Emad Nasab in Damascus's al-Darwishiyyeh neighbourhood. Soon after that, he was arrested by the police and taken to an abandoned building where they gave him a beating, leading the country to finally break its forty-year silence... Lastly, many more headed over to al-Hamidiyyeh market to demonstrate, then to al-Hariqah square in what came to be named the al-Hariqah protest. As one big heart, they walked and chanted slogans calling for freedom. 'God... Syria... freedom, that's it!' and 'The Syrian people won't be humiliated!' They were approaching the Ministry of Interior and the central police directorate building when they ran into security forces who proceeded to arrest a bunch of them at random. Regime supporters emerged, infiltrated the demonstrators and shouted their own slogans, which led to the end of the protest.

The next day, another group of protestors tried again. Armed with loud voices, they set off on the same path and went to the Ministry of Interior again. They assembled in Merjeh Square, chanting their slogans and calling for the downfall of the regime. That didn't last very long though, as security forces infiltrated the demonstrators, arresting some of them and dispersing the rest.

The Day of Rage

15 March 2011

It was inevitable that the volcano would erupt, having seethed for so long. And when it happened, right when the lava reached the crater before turning into ejecta, the moment of the blast required a name that indicated its innermost significance: that name was 'The Day of Rage'.

Activists went out to demonstrate all over Syria, responding to the general calls for protest. Although I'd never thought that the wall of fear could be brought down, I was overjoyed. After hearing what had happened in Daraa, and once the movement spread around the country, I rejoiced over my people finally speaking their minds, finally realising that they had a voice and that they could speak, not just whisper. They could shout. At last, something triggered the Syrian population in its entirety. Something unified their course into one single wave pushed through by conscience.

All it would take was a little flare for a bigger blaze to spread. Indeed, the events that took place in Daraa kindled the Revolution's fire and carried its flame from the furthest southern tip of the country, stirring people's moral virtues, galvanising their spirits and filling them with resolve.

Facebook was still not permitted in Syria back then, and I didn't have an account, but I was determined to follow the calls for demonstrations and to keep up with the developments on the Revolution's websites. The next call invited people to gather in solidarity with the people of Daraa in Martyrs' Square in Homs (commonly referred to as the square of the clock by locals), for what was named the Friday of Dignity. I memorised this sentence and I made up my mind. I went to the demonstration with a mind full of doubts about what would happen.

I didn't think too much about it. Martyrs' Square is on Shukri al-Quwaytli's street, where a tall tower stands in the middle topped by four dials on each side. It was only obvious to go pray in the mosque nearby the square and join the demonstration shortly after the prayer.

So, I went to the Droubi mosque in Homs and performed the Friday prayer. Naturally, the sermon was delivered in accordance with the Assad regime's instructions. The imam spoke in praise of the current conditions in the country, occasionally making nationalist references in his speech. As the prayer was coming to a close, a man stood up among the prayers and exclaimed, 'Glory to our brothers in Daraa! Allahu akbar!' His high-pitched voice sent shivers through the crowd, who soon shouted after him, 'Allahu akbar! Allahu akbar!' I was with a friend that day; we shouted, 'Allahu akbar!' as well as 'We sacrifice our blood and our souls for your sake, Daraa!' ... 'God... Syria... freedom, that's it!'

Our voices filled the mosque. As we shouted at the top of our lungs and encouraged one another, suddenly someone shut the mosque's main door. We found ourselves surrounded by the congregants who'd been standing at the back. They were members of the security forces, who waited for us to make a move so they could dampen our voices and stop the revolutionary contagion from spreading.

The cops bellowed at us, asking for the guy who had shouted first, until one of them pointed in his direction and they grabbed him. They wanted to arrest him, but we raised our voices again, urging every-one else to save him from their grip. An altercation between the cops and the congregants ensued; they hit each other with their bare hands until the young man managed to slip away. We felt the ecstasy of our accomplishment, which animated our conviction that we were doing the right thing. We felt reinvigorated and set off towards the square. Our slogans rose high, reiterating the peaceful nature of the movement and its demands. We were a group of twenty or thirty, but you could see that the other people on the street were with us in the way they looked at us. They were too scared by years of brutality to join in, but we kept marching, and we were thrilled because we'd just made the cops run away barefooted.

When we got to the clock tower, we looked like a small bunch against the backdrop of the broad square. Our voices vanished in the open air. That was the second lesson I learned at the very first protest of my whole life. A bad mistake, we shouldn't have met at the mosque near the square. Security forces surrounded us in full force while our hands were bare. Once more we raised our non-violent chants to remind everyone of our genuine purpose. Things got worse as security forces came closer to us. We shouted louder, hoping that the echo of our voice would keep them at bay. Unfortunately, slogans such as 'We sacrifice our blood and our souls for your sake, Oh martyr!', 'non-violent, non-violent, Islam and Christianity' weren't enough to deter them from hurting us. With these slogans, we were trying to distance ourselves from the accusations of racism and sectarianism which had been directed at protestors, as had happened in Egypt, but all that was for nothing.

They attacked us with sticks, electric cattle prods and I don't know what else. They beat us. To a casual observer, this might have looked like a scene from a horror movie whose images weren't appropriate for a general audience. However, the speed at which events were happening didn't give us time to analyse and understand. Some of us had convulsions and collapsed. Others froze and remained motionless. The only choice we had was to run, but even that wasn't as easy as it might sound. I tried to get out of the tight space where they had encircled and confined us, but one of the officers grabbed me by the jacket. We pulled each other and I zipped the jacket down, wiggling out of it. I ran until I was far enough to mingle with civilians.

On that square, there was a famous café called al-Rawdah. I sat at one of the tables and quickly ordered a cup of tea. A sympathetic waiter rushed to place the cup in front of me to make sure I wouldn't arouse suspicion. From the café, I watched motionless as men were getting arrested and shoved into police vehicles. How could that happen? How could I have been chanting slogans with them a moment before, and then next sit there as they were being dragged away to prison? How could the Revolution be squashed before it had even started? Why was it that Syria had no friends or allies? I couldn't hold the tears from spilling out, over the feeling of utter helplessness that flooded me and the people around me, over the sea of disenchantment in which the regime was drowning its people until they would become unable to speak or act.

I kept blaming myself for going to that mosque, which was too close to the square, but I also found comfort in the effort I made to go to the protest, even if it was nipped in the bud. Plainclothes shabbihah came in support of security forces and stood there with their weapons, bellowing their pro-regime slogans, praising Bashar al-Assad as their victorious leader, at which point my tears turned into sobbing. I placed my palms on my face to conceal the shame in my eyes, and my heart hurt over those large-scale calls to action which led to nothing but long prison sentences for some of us. Then what? How quickly the slogans calling for freedom turn into screams showing that the hangman still has the upper hand. With my head upon my chest, I wept over the dead Revolution. They say men don't cry, then they seek refuge in God from the brutality of men. Isn't crying the least we can do against that same brutality?

As I immersed myself in these thoughts, I heard some barely audible chants that mixed with those of the shabbihah. They gradually rose louder and louder until a river of protestors coming from all sides inundated the streets that led to the square. On their shoulders, they were carrying people shouting slogans that the crowd would promptly repeat. I wiped away my tears, got up and I pulled myself together. All of Homs was there in the square!

As the protestors arrived, tears and sadness gave way to joy and exultation. Security forces were terrified, and they receded to the margins, unsure what to do. I put down my tea and joined the protestors, chanting and repeating after them the slogans in solidarity with Daraa for a good half an hour. I was over the moon with excitement, walking among them. We were like one big beating heart again, one steady breath, one firm step as we crossed the earth with one loud voice that rose to high heaven. All this baffled the security forces, leading them to fire shots in the air. There's always a first time for everything, and at the square we were introduced to the whizz of bullets. I won't lie and claim that we acted heroically. We wobbled a little to make sure that nobody had been hit. Then they shot teargas and live ammunition at us, and the situation got difficult, to say the least.

Despite the bleeding, the heart was still able to beat. People shouted and cheered up each other. I remember this one guy that day and how he addressed everyone in a loud voice, inciting us: 'For the sake of your children! Persevere for the sake of their future!' Those words made a timeless impression on all of us. We had never experienced revolutionary activism. We were amateurs at chanting slogans, at dealing with live ammunition. We'd never seen blood flowing in the streets in broad daylight. Security upped their game and started shooting more and more. I came forward to provide first aid to the wounded as well as to some cases of asphyxia, to resuscitate people who had passed out, and to put bandages on injuries. I was putting into practice the things I had been studying at university, as though I had been learning them in preparation for this moment.

In a fit of uncontrollable rage, a young guy climbed over the door of the officers' club on Martyrs' Square and went on to rip apart the big poster with Hafez al-Assad's face. He kicked it, determined to destroy it, then completed the job with his hands by tearing the face apart, leaving half of it hanging loosely. In that moment, Hafez al-Assad's face looked as though it was admiring what this young man had done. Over the course of forty years, Hafez al-Assad was a source of terror for many, and tearing his poster was the best possible indication that the wall of fear that had separated everyone since the day they were born was coming down.

Soon after, the teargas dispersed us, and I went back to my place in my hometown, al-Qusayr. I was thrilled. The people – and I was one of them – finally spoke up. The fearless and good-hearted people of Homs did not let down their brethren in Daraa. My head was flooded with thought. I was all over the place until I managed to focus on two aspects specifically: the first was the creation of a field hospital to handle the cases during the protests. With the help of some friends, I organised the first such hospital in an orchard just outside al-Qusayr. We bought the necessary equipment such as gauze and plasters, as well as things like needles and thread that would be useful to handle simple surgical cases. The second aspect was this: making our voice reach the rest of the world, because the regime was capable of exterminating us without anyone knowing. Syrians were no less than people in Egypt, Libya and Tunisia. The wall of fear that had been in place for decades collapsed, and it was on its way to being destroyed. But before the rest of the world heard about us, our voice needed to reach the other Syrian provinces, first and foremost Daraa and its wretched children: we are here for you!

The main thing that occupied my thoughts at the time was how to keep the people's voice united. I was in a state of excitement, thinking about a way to contribute toward spreading the word. I considered sending a text message that would appear in the captions of one of the TV channels that supported the Revolution. It was only a few moments before I picked up my phone and sent the following message to Orient TV from my number: 'Homs: large demonstration on Martyrs' Square in solidarity with the people of Daraa. Security forces shot live ammunition leading to casualties and injuries'.

Can you picture giving a present to a child, making her eyes gleam? Or the way you feel when you see someone you have missed? Winning the lottery after being on the verge of total destitution? That's how happy I was when I saw my text message appear on TV. All I wanted was to spread the word, but eventually that pulled me into a flow that would give to me and then take from me, more and more.

After the first Friday of Dignity on 18 March, we began waiting to see whether the momentum would carry into the following week, which was marked by another call for a Friday of Dignity on 25 March. Throughout the week, arrest and intimidation campaigns took place, aimed at weakening the morale and dissuading people from going. Questions arose to which there were no answers, only time would tell. Will the Revolution be buried? Will our courage be defeated? Could our resolve possibly vanish? Or will the vigour of the protests mount?

I sent more text messages to the pro-Revolution TV channels from my number. This made it easy for some of the networks, such as Orient TV, to get in touch with me. They asked me if I was based in Syria, and they invited me to speak live on air. I hesitated at first... Could I appear on live TV this easily without getting arrested? That was the least that could happen to me. I thought about it, but I accepted their invitation to speak. I thought to myself, since we all respond to the Merciful (*al-Rahman* in Arabic), I would introduce myself as Abd al-Rahman. I made up my mind not to tell any lies and at the same time to achieve my goal of spreading the word. I introduced myself over the phone as an eyewitness from Homs, and I passionately related the events that had taken place in our city in solidarity with Daraa. That was the first time.

The First Glance

The protests continued, and they became the beating heart of the city. At one of them, I met Tarad al-Zuhouri. Don't ask me how, because it wasn't something that we planned, it was more as if destiny brought us together, as if our eyes couldn't see and our ears couldn't hear, and our bodies simply marched towards this destiny according to God's plan. That's how I became friends – or perhaps I should say brothers – with Tarad. Some thought it was odd for us to be friends, considering that he was some ten years older than me, but when two souls are so in sync with each other, they needn't ask about their age or what they look like.

I probably started this by just saying hello to him. I approached him out of curiosity one day as he was carrying his camera, documenting the events of the protests. That was back when the words would still get stuck in my throat when I spoke on TV. I told him my real name, Muhammad, and that I was in touch with a few media networks. This won me his trust and he started telling me about his work and his activism, which showed me first-hand the high aspirations that had been spreading around the country.

Later, we put together the media centre in al-Qusayr, where many others got involved: Ja'far, Muhammad, Husayn, Fadi, as well as Tarad and me. At first, I worked alongside them to save on the internet bill and to help them with their work, but soon we started eating, sleeping and going everywhere together until they became my new family, whom

I would see a lot more frequently than my own family and relatives. I looked up to Tarad specifically. All the time I spent at the media centre meant that I would accompany him to report on events as they happened. If sometimes I lost him or didn't know where he was, all I needed to do was go to the site of a massacre, a bombing or a confrontation with the police and I would find him there because he got there before me.

We were united by the same purpose. We started our genuine friend-ship by going to the protests together, then transitioned to the field of media reporting alongside one another, each in his own way. He would visit me at my place occasionally, and I would frequently reciprocate the visit. We decided that it was best to rent a place to work and spend most of our time together. Every time someone tipped us off before a police raid, we would make our way together to the orchards outside of town, increasing the sense of responsibility and fondness we felt towards each other. The risks we took to achieve the mission on which we embarked to deliver the news can only be described with three words: unity of intent.

I liked his attachment to his camera. He had cultivated it as a hobby before the Revolution, taking pictures of the great outdoors. What else can I say about him? Some people took to the streets because they were poor, others because wanted to uphold their own dignity. Tarad took part in the Revolution for everybody else before himself. He was well off, he didn't have to pretend he needed anything. But his love for his abased homeland, whose people had been degraded, was enough to push him to offer his strong physique, his knowledge of photography and his high-minded eagerness in service to the Revolution.

The day the first spark was lit, Tarad and his siblings left Cyprus, abandoning their assets which were split between Cyprus and Lebanon. Overnight the lens of his camera transitioned from capturing natural landscapes to shooting clashes with security forces, the smoke of bombs, the debris left behind by shelling and the limbs of the victims. His family had also had its share of sorrow: one of his brothers, Mahid, was a martyr, and two others had been wounded, one of them being famous for leading the chants at the protests.

Tarad was in his mid-thirties when the Revolution became his only occupation. He didn't care too much about getting married. He was already married to his camera. He took extremely good care of it; he cherished and adored it. When the Free Syrian Army was formed, he would always look at his camera and say to me confidently, 'This is our weapon'. Apart from this wife of his, he also had two inseparable companions: a cup of maté and his cigarette.

Once he won the Syrian national boxing competition, and when he served in the Syrian Air Force all he wanted was to fight against the Israeli enemy. His physical build was intimidating. He was of coffee-like brown complexion, cheerful and friendly, you couldn't help falling in love with him, he made hearts melt like cotton candy in a child's mouth. Although his physical build helped him run fast when needed, too much smoking caused him to cough after a run.

Someone like Tarad al-Zuhouri, a master in the art of happiness, was capable of finding hope even if he was surrounded by dead bodies and debris. He probably derived that from his unwavering and impressive dedication to praying the five prayers at their designated time. One is allowed to postpone their prayer if there is an emergency, for example, but that was certainly not like Tarad. He was like a father to me, a brother and a friend, and a call to prayer. He taught me how to recite the two *shahadas* in moments of danger. Anyone who met him can never forget that 'Bashar al-Assad, his army and his airplanes' can never change anything so long as he has his 'cup of maté and his cigarette'.

The Mask

Abd al-Rahman. At last my name was in the media. But that didn't last very long. It wasn't very smart of me to speak from a local phone, and it didn't occur to me that things might take a different turn. The first phone call was followed by the second, and the third... then I got the calls from military security. 'We know that you have been speaking on TV and that you call yourself Abd al-Rahman, we recognised your voice'. Reports had been filed about me. In the minds of Syrians, nothing is more ominous than the term *report* and its variations. In other words, this meant that I was wanted by the authorities and that I could get arrested anytime and disappear like those whom nobody remembered anymore. More threats ensued, demanding that I stop my revolutionary activism, particularly my conversations with the media networks. My family and I had no choice but to ask for favours and pay bribes to prevent me from being swallowed by the basement of some prison. On top of paying and supplicating, I also had to pledge never to do those things again. But how could I remain silent when I had a revolutionary volcano inside?

My New Voice

I thought about what to do again. My next step would have to be a lot smarter and more cautious. I decided to use a mobile phone with a non-Syrian number to elude surveillance, which was easy because al-Qusayr is located near the border with Lebanon, and I could pick up the signal from Lebanese networks. I asked one of my friends to get me a Lebanese sim card, which he gave me along with a new phone. Then I had to change my voice to make sure they didn't recognise me, so that I could pick up where I left off. I thought that if I put two fingers in my mouth while I spoke,[2] it would make me stammer and the words would come out weird but still intelligible. The other move was to come up with a new name under which to appear in public. I needed a name that wouldn't cause problems for me or anybody else. After careful consideration, I decided to call myself Samir. Samir Fathi.

How did I come up with that name? Where did it come from? I met someone with that name when I lived in Egypt, and I liked him. Also, because there was no one living in al-Qusayr with that surname, this choice was the least risky.

I started talking to the networks in my changeable, thick voice and with my new pseudonym. It worked extremely well and no one was able to find out about my double identity: one was that of a person who could barely go to the demonstrations and had only a superficial interest in the Revolution; the other had no face, only a loud voice that would spread the news of the rebels and of the protests through his phone and speak live on TV networks. I knew that I was playing with fire, and I didn't tell anyone in my family that I was Samir Fathi except for my mother. She was like a haven where I would take refuge when I had to disappear, and she made up an excuse for people in my absence, while I did my job. I was working secretly – I didn't tell anyone from the media office, not even Tarad. When I saw him for the first time with his camera, I became convinced that our goals were one and the same. The Revolution was ablaze, and we kept coming across young men with our same vision from all walks of life. I had a Skype account back then, under the name Abu Adnan, which had been my nickname for a long time. I used it to talk to friends and other activists from Homs and its surroundings, and we promised each other we would relate nothing but the facts, no more no less, day after day without exaggerating or misreporting them. I had eyes on every corner, and ears in every street, yet nobody knew my name. For them, I was just Abu Adnan.

Secrecy can be oppressive. Some of those friends were more like brothers, and I couldn't have done it alone. Some of them knew the truth about Samir Fathi. One of them was Bassam from Homs and the other was Abu Omar from Latakia, a city where I had previously resided as a student. I still avoided walking through police checkpoints by taking side roads, and if I needed to pass the checkpoints that were known for arresting the most people, I never took cabs or buses and used a friend's car instead. That's how I managed to get to the protests in Latakia, where I wrote banners with Abu Omar and joined other members of the revolutionary movement.

On the Verge of the Dream

By that time, I had taken up teaching nursing at al-Baath University in Hama. I used to drive from al-Qusayr to Homs to avoid the checkpoints where arbitrary arrest was most likely to take place, and then I would take the bus from Homs to Hama. We were approaching the city of Hama one day when we were held at a checkpoint. The officers asked for our IDs, and I was a bit scared. The guy sitting next to me winked as he handed one of them his card, saying to them, 'I'm one of you'. It was only a few minutes before they returned all the IDs... except mine. One of them bellowed to everyone, 'Wait!' Then that same guy turned to me and said, 'You too... wait'.

That's it, I thought to myself. It was bound to happen.

Half an hour passed while we waited; I was going to either get my ID back or be arrested. Half an hour during which I had no idea what might happen. Will they let me get to Hama or will my life stop at this checkpoint? That's it, I thought. There's no third chance. I peeked at the plainclothes officer sitting next to me, then I took out my phone warily to remove the memory card and throw it out the window without any-one noticing. Then I started deleting all the names and numbers from it, even the messages. Once I had taken all these precautions, the officer came back with a calm face and gave me my ID back. He wished us well and signalled to the conductor: 'Safe travels!' The only way to describe what happened to me that day is that God was on my side. Nevertheless,

I got the message. I wasn't going to be that lucky all the time.

The Revolution had been going on for six weeks when I had to miss two consecutive lectures. I was teaching Sundays and Wednesdays, and when they called me from the university on behalf of the students to ask me about my absence, I decided that, considering the situation, I had to limit my movements. After only six weeks, I quit lecturing. Right when the hard work was beginning to bear its fruits and I was starting to enjoy my relationship with the students, when my efforts were starting to inspire them, that beautiful chapter came to a close. I bowed out without saying why. The students still commended me. I established a good reputation, which hurt me even more in the end.

The Dead Quarter

In May that year, Bassam was arrested in his shop in Bab Houd in Homs. Regime forces had a reputation for battering the men they arrested and subjecting them to the most unspeakable methods of torture.

I learned that Bassam's phone had been tapped by the police. They found out he had been talking to Samir Fathi. Bassam hadn't brought up my name, nor mentioned my pseudonym, but they heard him telling me what to report to the TV networks about what was going on in Bab Houd. That was enough evidence of his association with Samir Fathi. At that point, the internal conflict between me and my other self reached a tipping point. They were torturing Bassam to make him give up my name and whereabouts.

Some defectors from the regime's army ranks had joined the Revolution without declaring it publicly. Security officers who supported the Revolution were trying to get in touch with me, however they could, to find a solution and alleviate Bassam's suffering. When I heard the news, I had been unable to think straight, pacing up and down, talking to myself and to the wall, hoping for an answer to come down from the sky and rid me of the enormity of worries that were tormenting me. While I was deliberating things, I found out that Abu Omar had been arrested as well and that the police suspected he might be connected to me. They tortured him too, expecting him to betray me. That was the last straw. I had never experienced anything nearly as disturbing and painful before, nothing that tormented my heart, mind and conscience so much. I had no other choice. I had to kill Samir.

After thinking it through at great length and having asked God for guidance, I knew Samir had to die. I phoned around and asked some contacts to get in touch with the media networks to report that Samir had died or had been murdered. A sniper shot him, and the police took his body, so he was gone without a trace. That way no one could have asked any questions about how or where it happened. And no one did. Al-Jazeera announced that the famous reporter Samir Fathi, a member of the Homs coordination committee, had been fatally shot by a sniper. Moreover, the Wasal network declared three days of mourning with a banner at the bottom of the screen announcing Samir Fathi's death, praying for God to grant him eternal peace. Similarly, other channels reported the news of Samir's martyrdom, mobilised their viewers, condemned the incident, and mourned.

Funny? Not really! On one hand, Samir was dead in name, yet he was still alive with his two fingers, his hoarse voice and the same confidence that he had fought hard to win from the TV channels, until he managed to prove that he was present on the ground at protests and at the heart of the action. On the other hand, he was now a ghost who could not show his face in public without causing more distress and trouble, or he might not make it out alive this time. Neither he, nor Bassam, nor Abu Omar. It was a weird feeling. Part of me was like a spirit, hovering over the remains of Samir Fathi's body, trying to figure out the meaning of his absence, while everything was slipping through my fingers. Samir died before his time, which made it even more necessary for him to rise again.

My only comfort was that Samir's death was not in vain, because it alleviated Bassam's suffering. They no longer needed to find out Samir's identity as he was never going to talk to news networks again. Sometime after that, through some acquaintances and by means of a bribe, Bassam left prison. Abu Omar was transferred from Latakia to a civilian prison in Homs, where they lessened his torture and the interrogations ceased. He was released towards the end of 2014.

Then we were back where we started.

The events in Homs kept making the news, due to the extent and the gravity of what was happening and thanks to the tireless efforts of the young men who reported the events from under fire. I felt extremely guilty to be sitting on my hands. I had already used up two chances. I put my family and my relatives at risk the first time when I was calling myself Abd al-Rahman and used my own voice. The second time I killed a part of me, Samir Fathi. Modifying my voice by sticking two fingers in my mouth again was not going to work. Time and again I tried and failed to modify my voice. I looked for another way to change it on TV, but I couldn't find anything. Someone told me that recordings on TV could be modified after they had been recorded, but not as you were speaking.

The Orontes's Debt

No matter how careful I was trying to be, I had to move around because of my new job as a reporter, to be able to go to those areas in and around Homs that had risen in Revolution such as Baba 'Amro, al-Khalediyyeh, al-Bayyadah, al-Qusour, Dayr Ba'lbah, Bab al-Siba', Bab Houd, Bab al-Drayb, al-Zaytoun, al-Rastan, Talbiseh and many others – the city with its seven gates and its streets had rebelled in its entirety. Every day, evening protests would culminate with protestors killed or injured. It became clear to us that we had a long way to go and that we had to honour their sacrifice!

The regime forces moved frequently those days because they weren't capable of occupying the entire city and they were confronting an erupting volcano, people who were coming out of the regime's grip at last after remaining silent and motionless for too long. That same army tirelessly battered its people. In September 2011, it was al-Qusayr's turn. The army attacked the city and carried out one of the worst massacres, murdering fourteen of our best young men by the banks of the Orontes River, almost as a payback to the river that had quenched the city's thirst for so long.

The blood of my friends Ma'in and Abd al-Jawad, as well as that of many others from my city who gave their lives, solidified the resolve of its people who became even more determined to hold their ground no matter what happened. The Orontes River, that the people of al-Qusayr revered, became more of an object of veneration, for its water was now diluted with the blood of their brothers.

Birth

I was back to square one again. Having become exempt from my teaching commitments, I settled down in al-Qusayr. I visited various areas in Homs driving through narrow streets to avoid checkpoints.

After Samir's necessary sacrifice, some ten days later, I decided that the best solution would be to get a mobile phone that could alter my voice as I spoke. The available technology was not exactly cutting edge, and the best thing I could find was an app, available both for computers and mobile phones, that could modify the voice after recording it. Getting hold of one of these phones wasn't very easy at a time when the market was inundated with Nokia products. I looked and looked until I heard about a device from China that met my needs. I asked my cousin Usamah – may God have mercy on his soul – to procure me one from Lebanon. I was only able to get one second-hand, but it did the job. As soon as I put my hands on it, I inserted my Lebanese sim card, and I embarked on a new phase.

'How should I introduce you?'

'Hold on a second…'

'We're going live in a few seconds, quickly please'.

'Fine. Hadi'.

'And your surname?'

'Hadi… Hadi Abdullah!'

The opposition to the regime hadn't established any liberated areas yet, and it would have still been dangerous to reveal my full identity in public. When I say dangerous, I don't mean only that it would've put my life in danger, but also the lives of my relatives and friends who had nothing to do with it. They could've used them as pawns to intimidate me. With the help of my mother, I thought of a name that wouldn't put anyone at risk, a name that couldn't be suspected of being connected to me but would merely serve as a cover for my activism now that I was able to change my voice on the phone. We couldn't come up with anything though, and when I got the call from the TV channel, I gave them the first name that came to my mind.

Although it came to me by coincidence, the name quickly stuck over the days that followed. In a moment of haste, I transformed from Muhammad to Hadi, everywhere except within my small family. More precisely, I became Hadi Abdullah.

From the very first day I joined the protestors, my family was always my greatest concern. And when death became a common scene, snatching friends one after another, I realised I was also a target and that the only choice was to walk toward it bare-chested. There was no turning back.

The regime threatened activists through their families, arresting women as hostages until the wanted ones turned themselves in. And for those swallowed by a prison cell, it could just as well mean... that they would never return. Thus, the nightmares only deepened, with the haunting fear that someone might hurt them.

You Guys Are Educated

When the first defections from the national army started and the insurrection was becoming militarised, the protests were still the main catalyst of the Revolution. Every day we went out in al-Qusayr and shouted as if in compensation for all those years that we had spent in silence. Our brothers and sisters in most Syrian cities did the same. As soon as the night fell, people would flock to the streets like stars filling the night sky.

Once I was at a friend's place in al-Qusayr. We decided to go out and live stream the protest on the condition that it would happen from his account. We went to meet my friend Dr Yasin Jammoul. My friend took off on his motorbike, whereas Dr Yasin and I rode another motorbike. Back then al-Qusayr hadn't been liberated by the opposition yet, and weapons were circulating among local people to defend themselves during protests. Riding motorbikes was the best way to avoid the checkpoints and to get away in case we were being chased.

I was driving. Dr Yasin was sitting behind me, and we were about to enter a safe area, despite being close to a military station. Suddenly, we heard rifle shots coming from the dark, like in the movies, and we found ourselves faced with their muzzles pointed right at us from all sides. Army officers had been hiding in the dark beneath the trees, and we couldn't see them. They halted us, ordered us to turn off the engine and raise our hands. We stopped our motorbikes in bewilderment. It was a mobile security checkpoint. Our hands almost touched the sky.

They took us – they dragged us – to the military security branch. They led us by force, as if we were ever going to refuse, surrounded as we were by their rifles. I was wearing a tracksuit, and in the pockets of my jacket I had a sim card for Thurayya (a mobile satellite service provider in Dubai) plus a mobile phone with a Lebanese sim card in it, which I had been using for most of my calls because it could alter my voice, as well as a Syrian mobile phone. What made things even more dangerous was the fact that I also had a piece of paper where I had been making a note of events, to be able to remember what happened when I was speaking on TV in case one of the networks called me.

That's it, I thought, things have come to an end. As soon as one of them puts their hands in my pockets, the next thing, my head and Dr Yasin's will be on the guillotine. He also had a cell phone with a Lebanese sim card in it, but he didn't use it to speak on TV, only for emergencies. That's when I learned what it is like to sense that you're going to die. I just accepted that it was the inevitable end.

They took us to the colonel's office, a room full of chubby officers who looked ready to go to battle. They were wearing helmets on their big, shaved heads and had thick moustaches. One word can summarise their terrifying looks: shabbihah. They made us stand in the middle and they encircled us before the interrogation began. They asked us our names, our jobs and who we worked for. Meanwhile, I tried hard to put a hand in my pocket and slip the piece of paper through a hole, but every time I tried to unzip the pocket, one of them would point his rifle at me and indicate for me to raise my hands. I tried to pretend that I was fiddling with the zipper, but soon I understood that doing that would give away that I was hiding something.

Once the colonel heard our names and our jobs, the tone of his voice improved a little, and the fact that we were university lecturers also softened the insults and the abuse, but they continued to interrogate us. A bunch of them left the room when they heard shots coming from the outside. They were scared that someone might attack the station, but their leaving the room also resulted in a more relaxed atmosphere. One of the officers took our IDs and ran the usual routine checks. The colonel said we both participated in the protests, which we denied. He insisted, though, and pointed at some reports that proved what he said. We remained silent. The reports were a point of no return. 'You're educated', he said. 'Your duty is to perform your role as enlighteners, not to drag the country down the drain'. We kept our mouths shut. Give me your mobile phones, he said. Every time we thought the worst part was over, we were confronted with a bigger threat... as though we were hanging in a pitch-dark basement where no shred of light could enter.

First, I gave him my Syrian mobile phone. He opened it and went straight to the messages. The first one he found was a text from one of my university colleagues which read 'May God protect you'.

'Why would he write "May God protect you"'? said the colonel.

'We both teach in Hama', I said. 'It's a dangerous journey, that's why we usually wish each other well'.

The guy who sent me that text was from Daraa, but I didn't tell the colonel about that because Daraa was on fire back in those days.

Then he checked the videos. He opened the first one, a song paying homage to Muhammad Matar – may God have mercy on his soul – a martyr from al-Qusayr. He was fuming when he heard the song and hit the desk with his hand exclaiming, 'This is a song by the rebels!' He hit the desk once again.

'I don't know who this is by. I just liked the music and decided to save it', I said.

'Don't lie', said the colonel.

'I'm not lying', I said.

And as I kept denying the accusations and taking his loud insults, he moved away from the videos and inspected the rest of the phone. My appointment with live TV was approaching readily.

My Lebanese mobile phone was still in the pocket of my jacket. I was scared that it might ring at any time. I can't remember if the appointment was with al-Arabiyya or al-Jazeera, but it didn't matter. One ring would have resulted in our demise, because I had saved the numbers of the TV networks as al-Arabiyya 1, al-Arabiyya 2, al-Arabiyya 3, al-Jazeera 1–8, Wasal 1, Wasal 2... I had no chance of getting away with it. None. But I took comfort in the idea that he probably didn't figure I had another non-Syrian phone on me. Unexpectedly, I received a text message on my Lebanese phone whose screen glowed inside my pocket. That's it, I thought.

'What's that glowing?' he asked.

'A mobile phone'.

'Why didn't you give it to me?'

'I don't use it', I said. 'That's why I didn't give it to you. I keep it just for emergencies'.

'What emergencies?'

'Just in case I needed to call someone and there is no signal on the Syrian one when I'm travelling between Latakia and Homs'.

'Gimme', he said.

Death is what I'd be facing had the colonel pressed the middle button, which led to the names of the TV networks and the button above it which led to the list of calls.

He checked the media folder but found nothing.

He checked the texts and frowned, then he bellowed, 'You talk to al-Jazeera! In English?'

I swallowed my saliva. 'Sir, that's not al-Jazeera. It's a text from MTN', one of the main Syrian telephone providers. He showed the text to one of the officers.

'Abu Ali', the colonel asked him, 'is that true?'

'It's true, sir', he answered.

Neither of them realised it was a text from ALFA, a Lebanese provider. God had been on my side again.

They thought the phone was Syrian. They kept threatening and interrogating us until the sound of shots was heard again. They let us go because they had something more urgent to do than interrogate us. We looked at each other in disbelief. That piece of paper was still in my pocket and our phones were on the desk in front of the colonel.

'Can we take our phones?' I asked him. He nodded.

We took off on our motorbike, and I started the engine with all the determination I had. After a couple of miles, I stopped, which Dr Yasin thought was a bit weird. I wanted to prostrate myself in gratitude. 'You can do that at home!' he said. 'Let's get there, then you can do whatever you want.'

We made it home. It was a journey surrounded by death, with everything but death in it.

Our friends had missed us, and they had started to worry. This was back during the first wave of defections from the regular army and the beginning of the armed rebellion. We told them what happened, and they thanked God that they didn't know we were being detained. Any rush decision would have resulted in us getting killed with no hesitation.

The Inner Conflict

Sometimes I laugh at myself, you know? How the whole thing started with just a text which then became phone reports and live appearances on TV. From Muhammad to Abd al-Rahman, then Samir and now Hadi. Four individuals in one heavy life, monotonous despite all its noise and harsh despite all its momentum and achievements.

Beyond that, there are traumatic things that remain dormant then bubble up, and scars that cannot be hidden even by the best plastic surgeon. The real scar never heals... it stays inside, in your heart.

Hadi started garnering credibility on the ground, and his connections with the satellite networks increased. I say 'Hadi' in the third person because it wasn't me, it was a mask I used to wear every time I spoke to a news network. It was the poor imitation of the changing and gentle voice so many people loved. That voice touched them and caused them to shed tears when it made appeals for humanitarian intervention... with even my father.

Hadi opened personal accounts on Skype and Facebook using his full name, Hadi Abdullah, and he used them here and there for less than a year. For maybe nine months, I would call the TV networks and use my real voice, that of Muhammad. Then as I went live, I would switch to Hadi's delicate and somewhat child-like voice. Back in those days, Hadi's voice would emanate from the TV set in my family's flat on the ground floor. My father would listen to the latest developments to fill me in, all whilst Hadi was sitting in the flat above his in a room guarded by my mother. I used to listen to people's remarks and read their comments on social media, which only made me withdraw further into my secrecy.

I had mixed feelings. Sometimes I would rejoice at the people's love and the impact that my reporting was making. Sometimes, though, I felt badly because I was concealing the whole thing from my father and siblings. But I would've kept it secret from my mother too – had it been possible to do that – because of how dangerous things could get if word got out. To make things worse, the regime positioned its checkpoints between different areas to prevent people from forming big gatherings. Protestors had to stay in their own areas. The fact that I didn't go out to protest bitterly disappointed my father.

The Confession

When the first areas in Syria were liberated and fell under the control of the Free Syrian Army, I began to feel under pressure to reveal my identity. It didn't make sense for activists, doctors and defecting officers to come out to the media while Hadi was hiding behind a child's voice. The Syrian networks Addounia and al-Ikhbariyyah spread rumours about Hadi Abdullah being a fictional persona invented by al-Jazeera or a Qatar-based reporter, therefore unable to report about what they referred to as alleged massacres taking place in Baba 'Amro, Karam al-Zaytoun and other such areas of Homs. Hence the question: why doesn't he come out in the open?

I was going live again. Shall I show my face and speak with my voice? What would happen to my family and relatives if I did? I'll leave it to them to decide, I thought, they're the ones who'd be most affected by anything I say or do, by any decision I make. Eventually, I had to confront my father and tell him the truth.

While I thought about the best way to tell him about Hadi, I was overcome with guilt. How could a son keep something like this from his father? I saw him in front of the TV listening to Hadi and praying for him to remain safe. I had told myself that I needed to keep it a secret for his own safety in case he got arrested or he let the wrong word slip.

'Dad, I'm Hadi'.

'Hadi? You mean Muhammad?'

'No, I mean Hadi'.

'…!'

'Hadi Abdullah, the one you listen to on the TV and the radio, that's me'.

'But his voice…'

'His voice is modified… I'm Hadi'.

I confessed to him. He was thrilled, happy and proud of me at the same time. He was also just as happy to be let in on this secret of mine as I was to unload this burden. I detailed to him everything that had happened since the beginning. I told him I was under pressure to come out in the open and that this would put him and the whole family in danger. The army might bomb our house, and we'd be more likely to get arrested, particularly because I was already wanted by the Assad regime. Despite all that, their faces were still gleaming with enthusiasm, as though my confession had come as a sort of atonement for my lack of attendance at the demonstrations. My father always used to say, 'Those who're going out are no better than you', while I followed the events of the protests in the rest of Homs.

The Confrontation

Al-Qusayr, 12 April 2012

'*As-salamu alaykum*. Yes, ma'am, my name is Hadi Abdullah, the spokes-person for the Syrian Revolution General Commission.[3] I feared for my family – that's why I had to modify my voice. We all know the criminal nature of this regime and that they take revenge on the families of activists if they cannot put their hands on them. My family have now made their way safely out of Syria, and I can finally appear live and speak in my voice'.[4]

'Are you concerned for your own safety, Hadi?'

'Ma'am, we await death as we await victory. The whole world must understand that the Syrian people have brought down the barriers of fear. We're no longer afraid. I myself have been travelling from one area to the other for six months without a stable residence'.

It was a new beginning. I immediately announced that my family had fled to Jordan. I wanted to keep them out of this, and I didn't want the regime to think that they'd be able to hurt my family. The regime bought it, even though in reality, my family didn't go anywhere.

From that moment, the live interviews on TV became field reports and special coverage. This increased my credibility dramatically, as well as my workload and sense of responsibility.

After getting rid of Samir in the past, the regime wouldn't miss the opportunity to put their hands on Hadi, especially now that he had a face and a voice. Now that they also had proof of my presence on the ground, I became more of a target because my work had a strong impact on public opinion. In addition, there was the curiosity of people who were against the regime as well as of those who had previously doubted my actual presence inside Syria. Until I showed my face, they'd call me 'the nameless reporter who became a target under the regime's fire'.

I warned my parents once again about the risks. I had to stay away from their house in order not to arouse suspicion about their presence in al-Qusayr and my relationship with them. I would only visit them occasionally.

Back then, the regime was our only enemy – there were no other internal foes. They were doing their best to be a constant source of uneasiness for people. Suddenly, your life is less important in comparison with that of your loved ones, and you start wishing for your own death to save them from the hands of torturers. I would rather suffer than live with the guilt of having stayed silent.

In late 2011, my uncle Hamzah, to whom I was similar in age and very close with, was arrested. We didn't hear anything about him after that… if he was dead or alive. Every time I saw my grandma, she would ask me insistently about him and if I'd been able to locate him… I could only cry out my frustration, another scar on my heart.

My grandparents' house, how can I possibly describe it? If you have grandparents of your own, I'm sure you can relate. In the first years of my life, I spent most of the time at their house. This made me very close to them because, in a way, they raised me. I loved them to pieces. My grandmother used to spoil me. The war made me fear for her and lose sleep over her safety and that of my grandfather's. I visited them every few days to check their blood pressure as well as their glycaemia. As a nursing graduate, I was responsible for their health and for bringing them everything they needed, including their medicine. The worst part was seeing them terrified by the bombing, and although bombing doesn't differentiate between old and young as it kills, and breaks and injures indiscriminately, I guess the elderly feel it in their own unique way.

Amidst this rollercoaster of feelings, torn between fear and helplessness, they still tried to make me feel that they were proud of me, especially when they heard my voice on Monte Carlo Addoualiya Radio and the BBC, or when they saw me on TV. They were particularly delighted to hear people talking about me, which pushed me to persevere even though I knew that there was no way back from the road I was taking.

In Heaven, Under Fire

In al-Qusayr, I spent most of my time doing media-related work in an effort to unify the different military factions. I had a good relationship with all of them, which helped. On the side, I was juggling my duties towards my extended family and my work.

Al-Qusayr

Can a word capture pain? A homeland? A life! What can I say to you about its roads flooded with memories that engulfed its sewers, inundating the Orontes River and its floodplains with bitterness?

If you ask me whether it's a city, I'll say to you: it's a city and a village, and on top of that, it's a garden and a home. It's surrounded by eighty-five villages that fall within its district. Orchards of apple, apricot, cherry, almond and other fruit trees cover part of its territory. The rest is occupied by one or two-storey houses spread across it, with only a few high-rise buildings. Its main market serves the local population, and there is a clock tower in the middle of its central square which came to be known as Saydah 'A'ishah Square, the same square where the Revolution's heart started beating for the first time. Its roads are neither broad enough for lovers to lose each other, nor narrow enough to smother their affection. As for the nostalgic feelings associated with the big family houses, they represented something special to everyone who lived in al-Qusayr and never came back.

I was living with my brother Shadi in a densely populated area, staying in an apartment that belonged to our cousin. Our close friends there would visit us regularly, especially Tarad, who was with us most of the time. Since it was easier for him to go around, Shadi was in charge of the logistics. He was our driver, and he did the shopping. He's three years younger than me and stayed with me until the turning point of the war in the Battle of al-Qusayr, during which he joined the ranks of the rebels to make up for the shortage of men.

I used to go back to that flat after finishing work at the media centre in al-Qusayr, where five or six others worked: the cameramen like Muhannad – may God have mercy on his soul – and Tarad, and the producers Ja'far Abu Habib and Fadi, under the supervision of Abu Shamso. Because of my media activism, I was a likely target as I moved between the flat and the media centre.

My next-door neighbour was my other cousin, who lived with his wife and their four children, the youngest of which – Rahaf and Sa'd – used to visit me every other day. They used to gleefully pop up at my door. Their smiles melted my worries away and I was able to blow off some steam. Did I mention that they looked like angels who come down to sweeten our existence? The sound of their laughs resonated in our flat and dispelled its gloominess, like pebbles thrown into the water, forming a ripple that echoes their impact. They felt at home entering our flat, followed by their father, whom they preceded eagerly. For my part, I kept cookies and sweets at the ready to make sure I didn't let them down in the event of an unexpected visit, and I took pictures of us together to capture those lovely moments we shared.

One day at the flat, I heard a tremendous noise and rushed up to the rooftop of the building to find out what was going on. I went for my camera because I wanted to document what was happening, but in the blink of an eye, before I could raise my head to point the camera in the direction of the bombing, I was blown away by the shock wave of an explosion. I was right near the bomb's target and the building across the road from mine had been razed to the ground.

Like after other bombings, smoke filled the air and made it foggy. The bombing struck my cousin's flat too, next door to mine. A huge rocket had levelled the house and blasted me off my feet. My nose began to bleed. I forgot about the camera for a second and focused on the smoke and the bleeding. Based on my experience as a nurse, I figured the shock wave of the impact must have caused vessels in my nose to explode. I stuffed pieces of cloth in my nostrils to stop the bleeding for the time being as I made my way to the hospital.

The shock wave shattered all the windows, making the place unlivable. Other houses in the area were also struck and their occupants as well as passers-by, got their share of shrapnel. As the paramedics were taking them to the hospital, I went with them and had to take the necessary precautions before I could return to the house. Once the bleeding stopped, it dawned on me that I didn't check on my cousin and his wife and children!

I spotted my cousin from afar, and I breathed a sigh of relief. Thank God, I thought, everyone else too must be okay. But then he asked about his family, and we figured they must have found refuge in the basement, so he headed over there immediately.

The only thing worse than waiting for someone who has gone to check for survivors is when they return empty-handed. He couldn't find them.

His two eldest children, he found out, were at their grandparents'. We thought the others might have made their way to the orchard because they weren't in the basement. After almost an hour of frantic searching, running from one place to another and asking around, my cousin eventually went back to assess the damage to his place. As he came closer to the rubble, the picture became clearer, and he thought he heard a distant voice. The tragedy was gradually sinking in, as though the initial feeling of shock had been dispelled and the reality of the situation became apparent. The whole house had been destroyed, and three members of his family were buried alive under the debris. There was no other explanation.

Where do we start? Which stone shall we lift first? Which wall shall we move to get faster to the victims? When you're racing with death there's no time for questions. We were all in a state of confusion with only horrible decisions to make; we had no choice but to start lifting anything and everything. The White Helmets did not exist back then, but there were other rescue groups available in such situations. A bulldozer that belonged to one of these groups was heading over to the site, but was struck by a shell and never made it to us. We got in touch with those in charge of sending the bulldozer when it didn't show up and found out from them what happened; it was as though they took that glimpse of hope from our hearts. We kept thinking and called around until we found the number of another guy who owned a bulldozer. This time not only was the vehicle hit, but on top of that, the driver was injured.

We had no other choice but to dig with our bare hands.

With the help of only rudimentary tools, we dug through the rubble. Just as thirst can only be quenched by water, our efforts would pay off only if we got them out alive. Tarad was digging with us and taking shots with his camera as well. My nose was bleeding again from fatigue, but rescuing those kids and their mother was all that mattered.

After over an hour of digging, Rahaf emerged from under the rubble. She was pale, and she had run out of breath before we could reach her. We took her to the hospital all the same. She didn't have any injuries that could have cost a little girl like that her life. Unfortunately, she didn't answer our calls, her heart didn't take pity on our tears. She chose to die with the least possible losses, in her house, clinging to her mother's leg, the only person she could hold on to. As for Saʻd, his hands didn't hold for very long. He didn't want Rahaf to go without him after experiencing the terror of being under the rubble together.

Then, we dug out their mother.

In the House

Suddenly before she knew it, it was as if the sky had fallen. It's impossible to know how painful this metaphor can be until it becomes fact, no longer conceptual but real. The roof of her house, their whole world, came crashing down on her and her two children and froze them in place. Even though we were all on alert for bombings and we kept hearing the sound of airplanes, it was difficult for anyone to understand what was going on in that situation. The smoke suffocated them, the debris weighed heavily on their chests and limbs and blacked out everything around them, except for a pale thread of light that penetrated, unnoticed. She could feel her children's hands clutching her legs, holding on to the last and only chance to save their lives, but that wasn't enough to let them breathe. Sa'd remained in this position for approximately twenty minutes. Rahaf resisted for ten more. Their mother couldn't talk, she wished she could speak to them even though they couldn't answer her. She wanted to tell them that she was by their side and that everything would be fine. She wanted to scream for help to catch their breaths and heartbeats before they stopped. She couldn't, and no one came.

Children idealise their mother as the person who has an answer to every question, a solution for every problem. In that situation specifically, though, her sheer helplessness emerged. She could barely breathe through an opening in the rubble though she wasn't able to share it with Rahaf and Sa'd. She wasn't more than another wall brought down by the airstrike, and for the children, she was just their final rest. Her body was riddled with fractures and contusions, her heart pierced forever by loss.

A Stranger in Our Homes

The day al-Qusayr became one big military camp, its revolutionaries had no choice but to pick up weapons to defend themselves as its neighbourhoods were being separated from one another and the city became segregated from its orchards. The checkpoints mushroomed around the city in an attempt to suffocate it, but that had the opposite effect of swelling the ranks of the Revolution and of galvanising the morale of its men. The shackles were certain to be broken now that patience and perseverance had taken root.

Tarad and I were covering the battles for the media in those days. The rebels started trying to rid the area of the regime's asphyxiating grip by taking control first of the checkpoints that separated different areas of the city, then of those that kept the city shut off from its countryside, which required an enormous military effort. Despite the magnitude of the task, the rebels did it.

Then it was the villages' turn. The rebels set off, galvanised as they were by the recent success, and captured the checkpoints and the military barracks in the villages around al-Qusayr as well as the ones in al-Tell and the artillery battalion in al-Qusayr's countryside. Then they set their sights on the al-Dab'ah military airport and captured it too. Ultimately, they aimed at capturing Homs with their artillery and liberating it. They followed their plans to a tee, the more so since they were getting their hands on more heavy weaponry and tanks as they captured more and more territory. When the time came, they set their hearts on Homs and prepared for the showdown. One single military unit separated them from their objective; its name was Rahbah Qattinah. They figured that was their final obstacle before they could put an end to the siege of Homs. The civilians started preparing for the big day, while the rebels planned the liberation.

They headed north like one big human river. 'God be on our side' was their weapon. It was not going to take them very long to finish the job since all their military equipment was concentrated on one single objective: Rahbah Qattinah. In the meantime, the Assad regime was losing its grip on all its checkpoints as well as on valuable military equipment. All predictions pointed in the direction of another victory for the rebels, except this time their feat was going to be a much bigger one: the city of Homs. The regime wasn't sitting on its hands and, out of despair, they sought the support of the Lebanese Hezbollah from the south and from the west.

Hezbollah started moving towards the villages around al-Qusayr, which exerted a great deal of pressure on the rebels. Encircled from behind, our fighters had to temporarily give up on Homs and return to protect the liberated territories from the advance of the Party of God. The fighting was fierce, and the battle raged for weeks with great ardour, with both sides claiming to be fighting in the name of God, except God *knows the wrongdoers best,* as the Quran says. The battle went on for weeks. The regime's airstrikes tore the sky apart supported by Hezbollah's men on the ground, fighters whose ideology dictated that their struggle against the rebels was a form of jihad which would be rewarded with a place in heaven. Tarad and I continued to cover the events in detail; however, a lot of the international TV networks didn't believe us when we told them about the presence of Hezbollah fighters. The information we had came from the Free Syrian Army units in the villages around al-Qusayr. Networks asked us to provide proof in the form of documents, fighters or prisoners. Telling them that we heard their voices speaking in a Lebanese accent on their walkie-talkies didn't convince them. This made us sit down and contemplate the best way to supply the necessary evidence.

The battles were extremely bloody. The number of men who fell on both sides was high. A Free Syrian Army fighter managed to snatch the body of a Hezbollah leader, which put us in a position where we could prove ourselves, expose them as a terrorist organisation and gain international support. We took pictures of the corpse as evidence and managed to find out that the man's name was Abu Ali Rida. Someone called his family from his Lebanese mobile phone, whose signal was available in al-Qusayr, pretending to be a member of the Syrian Army informing them that the man had been injured. I recorded the whole conversation without broadcasting it. Meanwhile, one of our friends in Lebanon took a picture of a death notice lamenting the departure of a Hezbollah leader which mentioned his name: Abu Ali Rida. This small detail was essential to complete the picture and for the video to be broadcast.

I kept the dead man's phone, and I started getting calls from people close to Hezbollah, one of them a doctor from the al-Zu'ayter family, who were getting in touch to negotiate and ask me not to show the corpse to the media. Of course, I refused to negotiate and asked them to desist from trying to convince me. The person I spoke to pretended to be a neutral party, but I knew he was in fact with Hezbollah. Tarad shot videos of all these phone calls, which I conducted on speakerphone, and they became further evidence that we could use in the future. They said they were ready to offer us as much money as we wanted in exchange for a deal. We turned them down and they upped the ante, offering us a travel visa to any country we wanted. Then they tried to buy me out with an open cheque, but this only made us persevere even more. We realised that the video was going to be extremely damaging for them. When they failed to persuade us with their propositions, the negotiators moved on and started intimidating us. They told us that they knew our names, our families and where we lived, and that Hezbollah fighters could hurt us.

Undeterred by their arrogance, we didn't give up.

Naturally, Hezbollah kept denying its presence in Syria even as it was fighting the Free Syrian Army in al-Qusayr. But the video, the pictures and the death notice were enough evidence to corroborate our argument. Arab and international networks broadcast the video, presenting it as the first tangible proof of their presence in Syria. This pushed Hassan Nasrallah, Hezbollah's secretary general, to appear in the media and acknowledge the Party's presence in our country. He also added that if there were a thousand of his men in Syria at the moment, they would become two thousand and that the Party's leaders were ready to take the field and fight themselves if necessary.

The Only Survivor

When the siege on al-Qusayr became tighter, and the fierce airstrikes replaced the clouds, the rebels defended us with strenuous courage and the number of injured started growing. Under the siege, medicine was in extremely short supply, and it was no longer possible to provide first aid, nor to get the wounded out of the city to receive treatment. We were getting between thirty and forty injured every day. Some of the most serious cases needed to be smuggled out of the city to save them, but we never managed to do that because, most of the time, the necessary movements involved running into a military unit. Then the food started running low too – flour and bread became scarce, and the warehouses were running out of everything. Families had to rely on relief deliveries, which soon became a mirage.

As an agricultural centre, the area around al-Qusayr delayed the threat of famine, making medical supplies our number one priority. There were multiple attempts to smuggle medicine in, but they were waylaid by land mines. Similarly, some of our cars were sent flying by landmines and the wounded became martyrs before we were even able to evacuate them. That's how we played our last cards, except our luck would soon run out. The siege was also increasingly exerting pressure on the doctors and the paramedics in the field hospital. They barely slept. What made everything all the more distressing was that al-Qusayr was the theatre of a humanitarian disaster whose cries for help never reached beyond the walls erected by the siege. At that point, rising to heaven became the best way to leave the city.

Shortly before the siege, one of the buildings had been converted into the only field hospital in al-Qusayr. All the doctors that had found themselves in the siege were now working there, offering first aid. I was documenting the lives of people living in basements, keeping a record of the wounded, the casualties, as well as military and political developments. I was going from one place to another trying to put together all the pieces of the catastrophe. The siege and the bombing caused the rebels to lose more and more men every day. My brother Shadi asked me whether or not he should join the ranks of the armed opposition, given that he knew how to handle weapons. I gave him my consent. He was my second brother to join them after my younger brother, Munzir.

One day I was with Tarad taking pictures and videos on the frontline, and as we were making our way back to my place, he suggested that we make a stop at the field hospital. I tried to dissuade him at first, but eventually I gave in. When we got there, I was shocked to see Shadi among the wounded. A rocket fired by Hezbollah landed near him; from head to toe his body was riddled with shrapnel, his feet and his legs were injured, and he had a severe wound in his stomach. In the throes of shock, I burst out crying and praying for him. On the way to the operating room, I took his hand and held it as though trying to save him from dying. He went in and so did I, in spirit. Death does not afflict the dead – it only deprives those who stay of their share of hope.

That same day I had to go back to the frontline to continue filming. When I returned, Shadi had been discharged, but his condition was critical, and he had to be evacuated from al-Qusayr as soon as possible. A day or two after that, my nose was bleeding again so I went to the hospital to get treatment. I noticed that people around me were whispering to each other. They were talking about the two bullets in the stomach of my other brother, Munzir, who is nine years younger than me. How could two bullets the size of my finger menace a body like that? It was as if the bullets liked the smell of his flesh. He had previously got one in his hand during the first peaceful demonstrations, which resulted in him having to spend some time in Lebanon to receive the proper treatment, although his hand never fully recovered. Now his stomach.

How did that happen? I could barely close my eyes before I had to confront yet another bad situation. They said he was with his friends trying to deliver some food to al-Jawsiyyeh, one of the villages under siege near al-Qusayr. As the first group of them was trying to cross into the village near one of the checkpoints, they came under fire. He went forward to help rescue those who'd been shot but in turn, he also got a bad one in his belly. He was in very rough shape when they brought him in, and because of the hospital's general state of decay, his situation didn't improve following an error during surgery.

One with his guts injured, and the other in desperate need of a lift out of the area to be treated. I was the only one among my siblings not to have been wounded, in a city surrounded by fierce fighting from all sides. And since death never stops during the war, my maternal uncle, Abd Al-Mula – who was more or less my age – also joined the list of those wounded, until he left al-Qusayr forever from his hospital bed and ascended into heaven.

My younger sister also had her share of grief. Her husband was injured in his face during the siege, which resulted in his disfigurement. My family's situation was difficult, and my parents were increasingly worried. They couldn't bear it for much longer. My siblings and my brother-in-law were smuggled out and made their way to the Qalamoun region first, then into Lebanon where they completed their recovery. While they were being taken out in a car, they thankfully escaped another attack targeting the vehicles that evacuated the wounded.

Throughout this journey of loss, despite losing so many, there was always someone in my life to live for... My maternal uncle died, my cousins and my friends died, leaving me both with a painful void, like a black hole in my heart, but also with cherished memories that kept me going. I continued breaking off tree leaves to plant them in my heart and nourish them with the water of the Revolution.

Exiting Paradise

Back when the rebels were making progress, before Hezbollah stepped in, it was difficult to even contemplate the idea of withdrawing. The battle of al-Qusayr was a pivotal moment in terms of both strategy and recruitment. Due to the external involvement by Hezbollah, the rebels won support from several Syrian provinces, although the siege's efficiency under the combined efforts of Assad and Hezbollah forces, together with the unfamiliar terrain for those who came from other parts of Syria to join their ranks, made it difficult for them to enter the battle. Only a few men from Aleppo made it through the land-mine-infested areas to al-Qusayr, under the leadership of Abd al-Qader al-Saleh, the young fellow with a brown complexion and a broad fore-head commonly known as Hajji Mari', and Abd al-Jabbar al-Akidi, a valiant man who was the head of the Aleppo military council at the time. They came with a group of fighters, among whom I remember my friend Firas al-Halabi and six others whose lives the mines took before they could join the battle.

You know that feeling when you're falling over but catch something to hold on to? This is what the arrival of the new fighters from outside al-Qusayr meant to us, an arm that bolstered us and a shoulder upon which we relied when things were tough on us.

The attacks were fierce, and the clashes were intense, but every time we were on the verge of defeat, the rebels always managed to pick us up and bring us back to the battlefield from which retreating or withdrawing was no option. Resistance was the only choice. We worked hard to break through the muzzle of the siege, but no one cared about our situation. We were steadfast, we were like candles struggling hard to remain lit to show the way to the civilians under siege... but inside we were melting down. We had to make a key decision to put a limit to the soaring numbers of people who were getting hurt.

A single field hospital was working round the clock like a beehive until they were so overworked that the place looked like a cloth saturated with water, heavy and burdened. The number of wounded was going up, and to make things worse, the hospital itself was bombed multiple times, but it managed to save patients and carry on. With every passing minute, things were deteriorating. There were way too few doctors for the number of injured; they were working overtime, and they knew that the fact alone that medical supplies were running low meant that the area was facing the prospect of a humanitarian catastrophe. Soon they would be unable to help, and the injuries would become necrotic.

Under the siege, the value of all kinds of goods was soaring, except the value of human lives. Fighters no longer feared for their lives as much as they were terrified by the idea of getting wounded, aware as they were that before they died, they would have to endure the pain of infections, ulcers and disease. Why not make things easier and greet death from the start with open arms?

There were fifteen hundred wounded in al-Qusayr and its surroundings. Food and supplies were running low. Medicine no longer reached the area, and death from illness or the bombs was the only way to leave for those whose bodies were failing. Retreating was very hard, but staying in that situation was even harder. As activists, we had to abide by the decisions of the military leaders, because ultimately, they were the ones who persevered on the frontlines of the battle, and they knew what was best for us and them. Naturally, many refused this decision, and although some were dying from their injuries, others preferred to stay in the motherland, al-Qusayr, until their last breath. Tarad and I were among the latter, a group of approximately a hundred people. We said that we would stay there until we died. We were like unbudgeable roots, like soil that would not erode from its orchards. How could we leave, when we were no longer capable of telling the difference between our memories and our dreams? When every one of us had concerns, and corpses scattered around that we were unable to pull from the debris... what other air could we breathe? What other land could support the misery of our pierced hearts...

But it didn't just rain. It poured.

'What you're doing is suicide. You can't stay without supplies or food... even if the least that awaited you was death...!'

June 2013, Facebook post by Hadi Abdullah
'The battle of al-Qusayr isn't over... we've had massacres and tragedies on a daily basis... unimaginable things that I can't even begin to describe... by God, we won't forgive anyone'.

We hadn't even said good-bye, and it was already time to leave. The evacuation took place at night. The last car left at six-thirty in the morning; tears flooded our eyes, and grief squeezed our hearts. If our houses could talk, one reproachful look from them would've been enough to make us go back... the guilt made us leave covertly under cover of night, so that at daybreak the place would look as if nothing had happened, except that our absence would give us away. Al-Qusayr remained a hostage that wailed as we departed, while our distressed hearts sank and implored for forgiveness.

We headed towards the outskirts of al-Qusayr where everyone had gathered, and from the rebel fighters we found out that we were going to have to walk. Fifteen thousand people, most of us civilians. We didn't differentiate between young and old, rich or poor – my grandparents themselves walked with us in the convoy of displaced people.

Members of the Free Syrian Army also walked with us, carrying light and mid-size weapons. Heavy weapons and artillery had been incinerated so that Hezbollah and the Assad regime would not be able to use them. The wounded were being carried, and we walked at the pace set by the children and the elderly among us, which meant that covering a distance of thirty-five kilometres was utter folly. In this journey of fleeing from the siege and the bombing, thirst and hunger were our two worst companions.

We set off from the outskirts in the evening, and we walked nonstop until the early morning hours. To avoid detection, we refrained from lighting cigarettes or using our phones and flashlights. And as much as that was tough on us, it was nothing compared to what we endured when we got to the international Damascus motorway. We were in a dangerous area, all of us in the crossfire. Our next move was akin to suicide: crossing it. To reach a safer area, we had no choice but to cross between two checkpoints sitting approximately one mile away from each other, and it had to happen at night so that they would not target us. When we got there, a new day had just dawned, wrapping up one of the worst nights of our lives. A whole city crawls out of its skin, then suffers from hunger and thirst in its outskirts... as though the land was telling us: come back, because you have no other home but me. ... But the tears soaked our eyelashes; we sowed the seeds of our own longing in the land we walked on, hoping that one day they would spring to life in the form of our return. Five in the morning, no chance of moving. For the first time, I prayed sitting. ... I was too weak, hungry and thirsty to stand. We prayed fajr sitting: Abu Firas, Abd al-Qader, Tarad and myself, then we all leaned on a tree and rested. The plan was to spend the rest of the day in the woods until the night covered us again, and among those deep-rooted trees we tried hard to unload the agony that had weighed us down.

At 7:10 a.m., escape from hell turned into hell. The sound of rockets sent shivers down our spines, the Assad regime and Hezbollah surrounded the woods and moved towards the civilians, two or three thousand people in each group. The more people gathered, the easier target we became for the rockets to strike.

And while there was nothing that the rebel fighters could do to alleviate our hunger and thirst, they did what they could to push back the soldiers surrounding us. They stood firmly by the few weapons they had left, but the splinters from this unequal battle hit us in the form of rockets and live ammunition. I remember Tarad's face very well as he said, 'What are you covering yourself with?' When I looked at myself, I realised what he meant – I was standing behind a thin tree trunk.

During six or seven hours, an unspecified number of Hezbollah fighters were killed, and three of their tanks were destroyed. In the same stretch of land that witnessed the tragedy of our evacuation, we buried twelve martyrs that had fallen under the bombs or during the clashes. They wouldn't let us bury them too far away. Tarad and I had been filming, and he asked me to give a speech.

'I don't feel like it... I can't say a word... I'm delusional... nobody will ask about us if anything were to happen to us...'

All the content that I had conveyed, the news that I had risked my life to cover, all for nothing. What difference was this speech going to make? He said, 'We film for the anniversary'. Which anniversary? Of what? Were we ever going to recall this? Will we still be alive anyway? And even if the camera made it out alive, would it be safe from the hands of the regime and Hezbollah's men? All my questions meant nothing to Tarad, who continued to film and to take videos of Doctor Qasim al-Zayn as he treated the wounded among the trees using rudimentary tools, a heart-breaking scene, to say the least. Sleeplessness, hunger and thirst clawed at my body. Which one was going to kill me first? Abd al-Jabbar al-Akidi tried to take the edge off, reminding us how Prophet Muhammad – peace be upon Him – also experienced the siege in his land and with his people, who also ate boiled tree leaves like we did when nothing else was left, after we had eaten all the almonds on those trees. His story would have made an impact had it been told in a different situation than ours. We were so tired and hungry, we didn't even have the energy to listen.

The night fell. We were at the end of our rope after such a long day. About an hour before midnight was the hour we'd been expecting. Crossing the international motorway was the hardest part. Five hundred metres from one side stood one of the two checkpoints, while the other one stood a kilometre away on the opposite side. Civilians had to cross while under fire from Hezbollah and the Assad regime. I tried to stand up, but I felt dizzy and collapsed. Tarad extended his hand and told me, 'I'll carry you'. I said no. I didn't feel I could walk, even if I leaned on him. I tried to convince him to go ahead without me, and that I would catch up with them, but Tarad refused categorically. I told them, 'I want some water then'. When 'Amid – one of the guys from al-Qusayr that I knew before – saw what was happening, he went towards the orchards looking for water and came back after fifteen minutes or so carrying a metal can which I suspect someone used for their cattle. In it, some of the water looked like... something else and smelled like cow excrement, petrol, or just a mixture of all things disgusting... but then, what's a bad smell when you're dying of thirst? My throat was so dry and thirsty that those few drops coursing through me were more delicious than honey itself. I had no excuse to sit, so I rose.

We walked in single file, a thousand wounded leaning on someone's shoulder or holding a hand, but the soldiers knew what we were planning to do and rained a storm of mortars on us. A fire broke out in a spot near us. Under the cover of darkness, no one knew what was hit or who got hurt. We came across a short rock wall and they told us that this was where the danger started. People were waiting for us on the other side and to reach them we were going to have to cross the international motorway as fast as we could. Crossing that road was a gamble, a shot in the dark – we could get hurt, or perhaps die, or start a whole new life.

A group of people went ahead before us, but when the sound of heavy gunfire resumed, the rest of us stopped. My legs gave out and I collapsed again. Tarad picked me up and carried me, and our bags too. That was more than the words 'friendship' and 'brotherhood' can convey, for someone's shoulder to become your crutch and have you closer to their heart... to hear their heartbeat and partake in their agony of letdown and defeat.

Crossing that road was a turning point, which forced us to move forward and leave the past behind. A journey of searching for a new home in Syria, in every part of the homeland which cried its sorrows to the one left behind. As you looked across the road, you'd recall the dreams you left in your grandparents' house, on your table and in your wardrobe; the streets you used to contemplate, wondering which one you should take; the faces whose features you didn't commit to memory because you never thought you'd part from them one day. What's more worthy of being remembered, before departing? Is it what's in your heart? The same one that will be consumed as time passes, though resiliently and refusing to give in? Why shouldn't you also carry with you objects whose smell can remind you of the people you hold closest to your heart, the same dear ones that will remind you of al-Qusayr, and rescue it from oblivion.

All my life, I'd always loved broad roads, except this time. This motorway going up and down in all its width was now just another chance for a person to draw their last breath. The presence of so many wounded behind us meant that a few had to attempt crossing the road before them. The people had been scared off by the shooting. I looked at Tarad and the other guys. With the little energy I had left, I said to them, 'Guys, if we stay here until tomorrow, we're going to die hungry and thirsty, the regime might capture us alive... if worse comes to worst, we'll die'.

During a war, standards are overturned and death, once the worst nightmare for the living and healthy, becomes a ticket to salvation. We took each other's hands fearlessly facing death and we ran, the four of us – Tarad, my cousin, 'Amid and myself – shaking off the last shreds of fear. We ran so fast we almost kicked our backs with our legs. We didn't even have time to figure out how much was left for us to cross before the bullets came raining down on us. The night, the sound of bullets, hands letting go, bodies rolling down, wounded and scattered along the road, moments that seemed endless. Between the tongues of flame from the sky on one hand and the gasping lips on the ground, those who were still running had no other choice but to look out for themselves. I lay down and blended in among the wounded, unable to help them, and I pretended to be dead. The four of us were dispersed, and I was alone. I was lost. I crawled as much as I could and reached the other side of the road. I felt so battered it was as if I was coming out of a hurricane... and what a hurricane! I longed for air as much as I had longed for water before. I breathed as if I hadn't breathed at all since crossing from the other side of the road. I don't know exactly where I stopped, nor who died and who didn't... the area wasn't safe, but it was free of gunfire. I was too afraid to move, fearing regime agents might arrest me. I had no strength left to resist if they caught me. I wasn't in any condition to even consider escape if it came to that. I rested for about fifteen minutes, then I tried to walk even though I was frightened as to which direction to take... So! Where should I go?... I was carrying computers and cameras in my backpack and fear in my heart about what the next few minutes had set aside for me. I was torn and uncertain as to what to do.

I put my fate in God's hands and walked until I heard a murmur nearby. I stopped. I tried to listen carefully to what was being said to figure out who they were and to what division they belonged. I hid behind the wall of an old, abandoned rest stop. I listened awhile until my waiting ultimately paid off when I heard them mention the al-Farouq brigade, calling out the names of its leaders in al-Qusayr, and I knew they were rebels. I went up to them, and they could see the signs of weariness on my face in the dark. They recognised me immediately; they took care of me and started yelling to each other, 'Hadi's here, we've found him'. They said they were going to take me to a safe area, but first I wanted to see Tarad and my cousin. I lay down and took a deep breath before I fell asleep, now that I had reached safety. Shortly after that, Tarad appeared before me. I rejoiced and greeted and hugged him – I couldn't believe that he was safe and sound. It was a few minutes before my cousin also joined us and we drank some water with the rebels. Tarad and my cousin told me they'd been looking for me for a long time.

The evacuation of al-Qusayr had death painted all over it, except our destiny was to go through separation, hunger, thirst, mortars and bullets, no matter how tight we held our friends' hands. We decided to go to an area situated on the Damascus-Homs motorway called al-Hisiya', and there we rested for a couple of hours. Then cars came to rescue us and eventually took us to Qalamoun.

Truce

I was filled with a sense of hopelessness about my media activism, I felt as if I were wasting my breath, and I seriously started thinking about quitting. I just no longer wanted to continue.

Tarad and I were in the Qalamoun region now, in a town called Qara, staying with a friend of ours. At his place, we were able to relax. We ate, drank and slept, and he bought some new clothes for us. After the second night, we moved to Yabroud where we stayed with Abu Mas'oud, the head of the local coordination group, and his family, who became our family too. Abu Mas'oud and his wife opened their door to us and, as they say, rolled out the red carpet. We became like brothers to their three children, Mas'oud, Suhayl and Wasim. We received the same treatment, the same food and the same clothes, even though having us in their house put them in great danger. People filled social media pages with questions about my disappearance since I had previously appeared frequently in the coverage of the siege and the battles. But what good did social media do for me during the journey of forced expulsion from al-Qusayr? What can media do for us while we're flooded with a sense of despair, with no one else to turn to but God?

It can sound meaningless when someone claims that people love them, but the outpouring of good wishes gave me a lot of optimism after I had lost hope in the role that my media coverage served. After that, we returned to our daily routine. I met my family, and they reassured me about the condition of my two brothers who'd been injured but were now receiving the proper treatment. Slowly we went back to our lives, while my brothers recovered. Munzer went to Lebanon to receive further treatment, and then despite the severity of the injuries he had sustained, he came back to Yabroud to heal. A truce had been declared, which was an opportunity to get away from the shock of the battles and the bleakness of the events we had witnessed. But every story has many chapters, as many as a tree has branches. Seasons go by and they grow, their leaves emerge and flourish until autumn comes again, bringing them back to their original gloom. After a few months, Tarad and I became bored and started wondering why we were still idle. Qalamoun was still in a relative and only rarely interrupted state of truce, which gave us the liberty to think about a place to pursue our activism. The Revolution was not dead, and we still had something left to give on the road to freedom.

Resumption

I started covering the battle of Mahin in the province of Homs, which lasted approximately two weeks, during which the local ammunition depot withstood fierce attacks at the hands of the rebels. One day, Tarad and I were sitting at the house of one of the families who had opened their door to us and was hosting us there. I suggested that we go check on the rebels to see whether they were advancing, hoping that they had succeeded in their attempt and that we could document their progress. In those days, we had been filming without releasing the footage, awaiting military operations to be completed successfully before we received the green light. We had covered a considerable distance on foot when we ran into someone accompanied by some injured people. He asked us for our blood type. I said A-positive, and he asked me to go with him to the field hospital to donate my blood for the wounded.

At the field hospital, they needed so much of it that the doctor had to take an extra amount of blood from me. He then asked me to make my way to our place immediately, eat and lie down. He even insisted that I shouldn't walk. As we were setting off to do as we'd been told, we received the news that the rebels had taken control of the ammunition depot. I looked at Tarad, unmistakably implying that we had to go there.

'What about the doctor's instructions!'

'We must go there, now'.

I didn't leave him a choice. A car took us to the depot where we were meant to go in and shoot videos. We had to cover a short distance on foot before we were able to start filming the concluding moments of that operation. I got dizzy, but a rebel vehicle drove near us, and I threw myself into the cargo bed. I shouted to let Tarad know that I would wait for him and get some rest in the meantime. It was the first time that I moved more than two meters away from him. I don't know how I managed to bring myself to do that, but I was probably too weak, I preferred to get ahead of him. And as I moved away and his image blurred, I heard the noise of an airstrike at which the vehicle stopped. I hid behind the jeep, I was about to pass out and I could barely tell what was happening. Tarad had been filming, and the vehicle was right in the middle of his lens. The rockets started raining down on the vehicle, right before Tarad's eyes. Thank God they were relatively small rockets. I got only some shrapnel in my skull. It was the first time I saw Tarad crying since I had met him. It was the strangest vision to describe and the best of feelings, to realise how dear I was to someone who was only just carrying me as we were being evacuated, and now was filming my injury, then a second later he was hurrying to check on me with a mixture of fear and affection.

I received first aid, my injuries were bandaged, and the shrapnel was removed from my head. Even though it had barely penetrated, my head was banging, but again I thanked God, as always.

We went back to the house to get some rest. I felt suffocated, I was going to explode if I sat a second longer when my duty was to be on-site to complete the shooting. After less than one day I set off with bandages on my head, armed with the desire to finish what I had started.

❖ ❖ ❖

'Joining us now from Homs is Hadi Abdullah, a member of the Syrian Revolution General Commission. Hello, Hadi. Hadi, could you give us some updates as to today's developments on the ground in Homs and its province?'

'Hi, the most important development today was the announcement made by the rebels in Homs and in the eastern part of Homs province that they had taken control of the ammunition depot in the city of Mahin. This is considered the second-largest depot in Syria. After ten days of siege and after clearing the area around it, the rebels were able to take it in its entirety'.

'We can't see you, Hadi... are you still with us?'

'...'

'I wanted to ask you about the weapons, firstly. Are you still at the depot? Also, we see that you're injured, are you alright? Were you there during this battle too?'

'Yes, thanks for asking – God protect all the Syrian wounded. I was indeed injured two days ago. I was with the rebels as they were attempting to attack the ammunition depot, but we were targeted by an airstrike carried out by the air forces in that area. Some of the rebels I was accompanying gave their lives'.

After my injury in Mahin, I returned to Yabroud where I received treatment for my wound, which wasn't very serious according to the doctors. Had it penetrated one centimetre further, I would've been dead, they added.

A Bloody Road

People always ask me about the secret of our revolutionary perseverance in the face of the massacres and the abuse. Many reasons perhaps can be encapsulated by one concept: we owed it to the martyrs. Maybe God wanted this Revolution to last for as long as it would take to bear its fruits. Did it not start with children writing graffiti on a school wall? Didn't it become stronger and stronger as the women of Baniyas stood in defiance in front of the tanks? Didn't its flames flare up and blaze across the country upon hearing the cries of the children slaughtered with knives in Karam al-Zaytoun and al-Houla?

Didn't we all caress our children after we had seen the images of Hamzah al-Khatib's body disfigured in prison by Assad's thugs? Didn't all the Kurds rise as one when Assad murdered their hero Mash'al Timmo? I could go on... every time the determination of the revolutionaries let up or showed signs of weakness, another, more heinous massacre occurred which reminded us of the brutality of Assad and his allies and strengthened our certainty in the righteousness of our path in the face of all the obstacles and challenges.

The Revolution is still alive ...
The Revolution is still alive, and we still have something to give on the road to freedom. We set our sights on al-Ghoutah, near Damascus. We asked about the best way to get there, and we were told that we

would have to walk. Fair enough. We were going to cross from western Qalamoun to the eastern part, pass through al-Rahayba, then al-Dumayr, before setting foot in al-Ghoutah at last. We didn't have other options anyway. Tarad and I thought that once we got to al-Ghoutah, we could stay a while. We would be close to Damascus, and we could witness the fall of the regime from there. We hoped to be able to help the Revolution from the heart of its most heated region.

We packed our things, then prepared ourselves mentally to bid farewell to my family and to explain to them in detail the importance of our relocation to al-Ghoutah. They were fearful, but they respected and appreciated whatever decision I took. We hit the road right after sunset. We plunged into obscurity, trying to avoid the checkpoints until sunrise. We spent eight hours climbing up and down mountains, it was one of the toughest experiences of my life. When we got to al-Rahayba, the fatigue seeped from our bodies like droplets of morning dew, but our guide's voice rose to our ears, reminding us that he wouldn't wait for anyone and that we couldn't risk being delayed or, worse, fall prey to the regime's thugs. After a whole day of walking, we arrived at al-Dumayr and had to find our way to al-Ghoutah again.

We started asking everyone we ran into to point us toward al-Ghoutah, which was under siege at the time, although the rebels there were trying to break the blockade. (They failed.) Despite all the people advising us against this because of the danger involved, we were determined to reach al-Ghoutah on foot. We had no other choice.

In the middle of a pitch-dark sky, a full moon smiled at us, which meant we had to stop and wait until it faded. Its light, a helpful companion for night-time campers, might get us killed this time.

There were about thirty of us. We desperately needed the pitch darkness and obscurity to be able to sneak between two military units – Division 16 and Brigade 20, as I remember. We had no sooner set off on our first day than they started shooting at us. It seemed that someone had tipped them off about our movements. We walked back to al-Dumayr without a scratch, already thinking about when and how our next attempt would take place.

Two days after that, we received the green light and were told to get ready. We started walking towards al-Ghoutah, but an ambush pushed us back before we could even walk as far as we'd walked the last time. Our hearts sank as we turned around and walked back once again. That was enough indication that we needed to change our plans. No bullet or bomb could deter us. We would try every possible route until we found a safe one.

For our third attempt – the hardest one – we were told to change the itinerary. We formed a single long file of thirty, maybe forty people, both civilians and Free Syrian Army fighters, and we marched for approximately two-and-a-half hours with high hopes of getting to al-Ghoutah at last after all we'd been through. I was the seventh in line, Tarad was behind me. Suddenly, we heard a huge explosion ahead of us and smoke filled the air. It was a few seconds before we heard more explosions, which made us all run and scatter around. The late hours of the night, together with the loud voices and the smoke, filled us with intense fear. As I moved away from the path we'd been walking on, I held Tarad's hand and asked him what was going on. Is it another ambush? Artillery? Landmines? All questions that remained unanswered for a good ten minutes until we found out that the explosions we heard were landmines planted there specifically to prevent people from reaching al-Ghoutah.

But that didn't matter at that point, because Tarad and I found ourselves faced with a more urgent task: locating our fellow rebels. There was no sign of anyone on the dark horizon, as if no one remained in the area but Tarad and me. While I was thinking about what we should do, Tarad pointed out that a group of people had passed ahead of us, which likely meant they had been injured by the landmines. He intended to move forward to help them, though we both knew that one wrong step would be enough to injure us as well.

Despite the danger, we began walking extremely carefully, feeling our way step by step like mice in a maze. After a short distance of slow, cautious walking and scanning, we began to hear someone shouting... then suddenly, the scene came into focus: six people and a lot of screaming. After checking one of them on the neck to see if he was still alive, we realised there were five wounded and one martyr. Most of the injuries were in the legs, many of which had been turned into mangled flesh. Even though darkness enveloped us, the strong smell of blood revealed the severity of the wounds.

I asked myself again, What are we going to do now? It was as if the entire war could be condensed into a single question mark; I didn't feel like there were any room for reflection, grief, or emotion, only a forced rationality driven by a struggle to survive.

Tarad and I were the only two who still had functioning legs, and the responsibility that came with that, especially with all those wounded around us, was as great as our lack of knowledge of the area we were in. We didn't know how to go back, or even if we should carry on to al-Ghoutah. But the more confused we became, the more certain we were of one thing: we could not consider any solution that involved leaving the wounded to bleed out.

First, we tried to carry the first wounded man back, carefully retracing our steps, but he was far too heavy for just the two of us, especially after walking for two and a half hours, which had drained our energy far too much and left us without any strength. What could we possibly do with our exhausted bodies?

We laid him down on the ground and reassured him we'd return, but our words didn't convince him. He kept pleading with us, begging us not to leave him. Then we found two young men hiding nearby and asked them for help. Just when we thought help had arrived, regime forces began firing flares in our direction, trying to uncover what was going on.

The atmosphere turned even more terrifying, and we feared an assault we had no strength to withstand. We began transporting the wounded, one at a time, ten meters back, leaving the only martyr alone at the front. We still had no idea where exactly we were, bracing for an attack at any moment, surrounded by wounded on all sides. Beads of sweat poured down heavily, while exhaustion depleted us of our strength.

This is the end, I thought to myself. The only difference now is that we have time to say our goodbyes and pray to God before breathing our last. I began reciting verses from the Quran, and we all cried. We all prayed. I spoke to myself about the tenor of our prayers and how it had to be a reasonable one. How could I pray to be saved while regime soldiers were nearly sealing off the sky above us? The ground beneath us was a sea of fire, and we would never know when one of our feet would land on a mine and end it all.

As I was lifting one of the wounded, Tarad motioned to me to be more careful so I wouldn't hurt him due to my unsteady grip and fatigue. The wounded man heard him and asked me, 'Who are you?' When I didn't answer, he pleaded for me to answer his question. He said, 'I heard him call you Hadi', and faced with his insistence, I told him my name was Hadi. But instead of stopping the conversation, he persisted and wanted to know my surname too. I said, 'For God's sake, just let me be!' I was carrying him as he kept talking to me. I repeated that he should let me focus and stop talking, but he was insistent like before. Then he said, 'Please, aren't you Hadi Abdullah?' The moment I said 'Yes', a surge of energy ran through his body. He lifted himself from my arms, kissed me on the cheek, and began showering me with words of gratitude and praise.

I couldn't hold back my tears as I smiled. He told me he had been the commander of a battalion, and that his men had left him behind. And yet, here I was, carrying him. I said, 'This is my duty', but he kissed me again, and I embraced him. Then I stopped walking, laid him gently on the ground, embraced him once more, and said, 'You are my brother. I will not leave you, no matter what happens...' A word from one man to another, witnessed by God the Almighty.

As for Abu Hamzah, the young man from Daraa who was heading to al-Ghoutah, he left me with a memory I will never forget. He was wounded that day. He looked at me and Tarad and said he was feeling cold at which point I took off my jacket, covered him with it and was left in just a cotton shirt. He looked at me and said, 'This is the end. I'm finished'. I cried and told him, 'No...' But he didn't wait for my permission... And who am I to give it?

He uttered the shahada and surrendered his soul, leaving his remains in my arms, his head resting between my forearms, as if I might warm him. Despite the overwhelming number of images of martyrs crowding my memory, and the wounded whose lives intersected with mine, Abu Hamzah was the first to die in my arms. Was it the madness of the first time? Or its uniqueness? Does everything really lose meaning when it repeats? Do people become numbers once they're part of the calendar's grim recurrence? Isn't death always a first time, every time, and isn't life itself the repetition?

Abu Hamzah passed away, and I felt the Angel of Death breathing right beside me. I began to cry more intensely, reciting Surah al-Mulk and praying for him. I informed the others of his martyrdom, and panic spread among the wounded. Fear gripped them as they sensed the end was approaching. I started thinking about what we needed to do next, and I remembered that the guide who had been accompanying us was supposed to be among the first five people. I asked about him, and there he was, lying among the wounded! I said to him, 'For God's sake, why didn't you speak up earlier? Do you have a walkie-talkie?' He handed it to me, after more than two hours of carrying the wounded! I asked him where we were, and he said we were in the Khaymat al-Safra area. Then I asked which channel the walkie-talkie was tuned to, and he replied that it was connected to the operations room in al-Dumayr.

I began calling out to the communications officer in the operations room – his name was Rida. I kept shouting his name until he heard me and responded, and I was overwhelmed with joy. I said, 'This is Hadi! Abu Adnan!' He replied, 'Yes, Hadi, tell me, where are you now?' I told him about the ambush we had been caught in and gave him our exact location. He asked me to stop talking because the devices were being monitored. Honestly, if someone had described that day to me, the events and the people I wouldn't have believed it. It felt like something out of an exaggerated film, or a plot written purely for dramatic effect.

He asked me to stop speaking and told me he would send help. Before ending the call, I requested stretchers for the wounded. No sooner had Rida finished speaking than his warning proved true, and a nearby area started to be bombarded. The walkie-talkies really were being monitored. But we had no other option. And as we waited for help, our fear of the regime's forces storming the area grew steadily. Even though I had suspected the walkie-talkie devices to have been monitored from the beginning, they were our last card in the game, and we had no other option but to play it on the battlefield, hoping it would bring salvation.

The young men began preparing to cover our retreat from the area, bombarding the nearby military post so we wouldn't be within its firing range. A military support unit joined us a little over an hour later. They tried to enter with their vehicles, but the terrain made that very difficult, so they advanced as far as they could and continued on foot. When they finally reached us, we couldn't believe our eyes. After all the fear that had consumed us and the terror that nearly tore us apart, the possibility of survival returned. The joy of that idea carried us into the hands of the support unit, who took over the mission. The young men retrieved the bodies of the two martyrs and transported them along with the wounded to the vehicles. We then returned to al-Dumayr at the break of a long-awaited dawn, a new page for a new chapter.

The psychological toll of that final attempt to reach al-Ghoutah was heavy. And while we were constantly grateful to God for saving us from certain death, we had lost hope in the possibility of entering al-Ghoutah. Then news arrived that the rebels intended to launch a battle in Qalamoun to retake al-Qusayr. That gave us the motivation to return. A few days later, we began our journey back on foot, once again crossing between military checkpoints, walking day and night until our feet were worn raw from exhaustion.

At around three in the morning, Tarad and I finally reached Yabroud. My family welcomed me with the warmth and love of those who had longed for our return, as I had told them we were coming and had stayed in contact with them throughout the journey.

My Eyes Hurt

Both Tarad and I woke up early. He had gotten up a little earlier than me, so he put on the maté while listening to Fairuz. He told me that his heart was telling him something was afoot... specifically, something unpleasant. I asked him, 'Why? ... what makes you feel that way?' I insisted, 'Does this have anything to do with the dream you had?'

The battle was raging in the area around Yabroud, and Hezbollah fighters attacked the city. I decided to change my media strategy. For a variety of reasons, I decided to quit live appearances on TV and focus on the events, mainly because I thought that appearing live on TV had proven pointless. Now there was going to be a single unified media platform that would broadcast all the footage, with the help of Tarad and the guys from the local Revolutionary Council in Yabroud. No one had to stand in front of the camera.

It was several days since the battle had started. One day, we were covering the attack by Hezbollah fighters in Rima, in the outskirts of Yabroud. The sun was setting, and we were hoping that the fighting would cool down a little. The guys from Yabroud wanted to split up and go back in different groups at different times, so they asked us if we wanted to go with them. We needed to go with them anyway, to be able to upload and share the videos on the internet. Tarad looked at me and asked me to go with the first group and said that he would go with the next one. I pondered this for a few moments, but I had no objection to it, as long as he looked after himself in my absence. I wanted to be extra careful and asked the Free Syrian Army lieutenant colonel Abu Ahmad to look out for Tarad.

A month earlier:

'He will become a once-was'.

'A once-was?'

'I mean one of us, either me or you, will be killed and die as a martyr'.

'Hey man, I had a dream two days ago, I lost my right eye. I lost one of my eyes. My eye was gone'.

'If it was the right eye, then it'll be me'.

'For the life of me, I can't remember which one it was'.

'Thank God, I'm not one of your eyes'.

'If it was the right eye, then it'll be me'.

'What's with you and this feeling that one of us is going to die? Didn't we promise each other that we'll live and die together?'

'Is it our decision?'

'...'

'Either we die as men...'

'We said that we'll live and die together'.

'That's up to God the Almighty, not you'.

'La ilaha illa Allah'.

'...'

'What do you mean?'

'I'm bidding farewell...'

He said that, then he laughed. I laughed too, as though the whole thing was going to remain a joke forever.

I went to our house in Yabroud and waited for Tarad to come back until someone called me from the field hospital and told me that Tarad was rushed in because he had been injured. How did I get into the car? How did I drive it like a maniac? I don't know. I felt my heart beat so fast I thought it would break my rib cage as I drove through Yabroud. All I can remember is that I got the call and then I was standing in front of his unconscious body. His eyes were closed, as if resting all at once after these years of fatigue. I didn't care about the bandages wrapped around his head, and there was nothing the doctors could do to stop me. It was all a big joke, and I was impatiently waiting for it to end. I tried to awaken him. I called his name time and again, hoping that he would recognize my voice, show me some mercy and wake up. 'What's the matter', I asked. 'Why is he not replying?' I gave up. I tried to lighten this up a little. 'Tarad what's with you?... answer me... stop it... answer me, love...' ... He never answered. All I wanted was a sign from him to say that I was right and the doctors were wrong.

They said he wasn't going to answer, and when I got frustrated with them, I started yelling, 'What do you guys know? Get off me!' I didn't realise what I was saying. Doctors' answers are only correct as long as they let us hope that the person will recover, and when they don't, we dismiss them and turn to God and pray. I still had hope, I tried to wake him up again. Since he knew me very well, Dr Saleh Sa'diyyeh came forward and hugged me. He tried to make me see reason and he calmed me, then he told me that Tarad's condition was critical. I couldn't bear the weight of his words. I pushed him away and told him that he didn't understand.... 'Tarad is going to make it, no matter what you say!' Everyone appeared to me as if they were conspiring against me. I was alone and helpless. My only friend was about to leave forever. I gave out and collapsed. The only thing I could do was pray to God; meanwhile, they decided to transfer Tarad to Lebanon. I couldn't believe what was happening. My vision was foggy. I sensed a vague atmosphere of hope around me while I groped around between reality and dream. They were like scenes from an endless nightmare. All my hands could do was turn to God and pray.

I wrote a post on Facebook asking my friends to pray for Tarad because his condition was critical, hoping that their appeals to God might save him.

He died five days later, on 20 February 2014. He was gone, and I couldn't say goodbye to him. God had decreed that I stay behind in this world and that he go to heaven first. That's how I deluded myself. To make matters even more disheartening, the rebels didn't manage to retake control of al-Qusayr... Tarad's family who were based in 'Arsal, in Lebanon, decided to bury him there. I was surrounded by the fighting in Yabroud, which seemed no more than a hug and a kiss away. I wanted to say goodbye to him, but it was too dangerous for me to cross into Lebanon. My extended family tried to dissuade me and warned me at length of the risks involved. I didn't listen to them, and I went. Having missed my first farewell with him, I didn't want to miss the second one too, no matter the cost. I crossed the border with Lebanon illegally. My tears preceded me. I went to Tarad's family, and I hugged them one by one, as if taking a share of distress off their shoulders and adding it to my own. I never stopped crying as I told them I wanted to be their brother for Tarad. Tarad's mother's patience was incredible. Together with the rest of the family she calmed me and consoled me as though I was the only one hurting. We shared the grief and meanwhile, Tarad's cold body was spending its last night in the morgue.

My cousin surreptitiously filmed the whole scene of my last goodbye to Tarad, of me kissing him and my last entreaty that he wake up from his eternal slumber. Later, as word had gotten out that I had crossed into Lebanon, I had to go back to Yabroud via the same route, which meant that I couldn't attend the burial and entered a long period of depression.

I cried all the time, and I didn't want to see anyone. I didn't do anything. Sometimes I would get up and shoot something with my camera, but without any desire. The regime took Yabroud, and the rebels retreated to the Qalamoun Mountains. A month had passed since Tarad's departure, making everything in life grim, blurring the meaning of all things and actions. To top it all off, we were staying in stalls three- or four-square metres in size.

When God put his body in that ditch, he also pulled me to the edge of it. I staggered on the brink between lingering on and perishing, drowning in depression, contemplating whatever was left for me... yet there's a long road ahead, and it is my duty to step away from the ditch, because my grief and my weeping are not going to bring the dead back. I had to move on and to continue delivering a message. I might as well keep the Revolution alive despite all the losses and hardships.

Part Two 2014-2019

A Journey of Longing

I was staying in the same room with my cousin and my brother. We didn't have access to a toilet, so after a while, I built one myself. Life in the mountains was tough, which meant that it took me longer to adjust to the feeling of loss. The only people we saw were rebel fighters, and I longed to meet some civilians. Given the situation I was in, meeting someone new would've been a source of immense joy. This meant that for months my mental health deteriorated.

On the other hand, the whole thing could be seen as a blessing in disguise. Thinking about Tarad, my love for him and my belief in the Revolution's significance served as an impetus to get back to work. I was aware that this would come at a cost, but Tarad wouldn't be happy to see our flag at half-mast. I pulled myself together and I was determined to carry on. If Tarad could see me, then he would only be content if I walked on the same path that we had promised each other never to turn back on.

Now that the fighting in the Qalamoun area was over, there was nothing for me to do there. If I still wanted to offer my contribution to the Revolution, I had to leave that desolate area. Otherwise, I would be just another guy sharing the news on his Facebook account, like any Syrian in exile.

I moved to the north of Syria and then to Türkiye in the utmost secrecy. I settled there and I launched a new show, shot half in Istanbul and half in Syria, called 'The Spirit of the Revolution'.[5] In the time between one episode and the next, short visits to loved ones made my days. But happiness, like everything else, never lasts too long. In one of the many tents that sheltered Syrian refugees in Lebanon, my grandfather's hopes of ever going back home came to an end as his soul ascended back his Creator by the will of God. A few relatives stood around his deathbed for their last farewell to the family's most senior member, except I was missing from the scene, a scene that would never be complete again after that.

A New Dawn in Kafranbel

December 2014

Since the early days of the Syrian Revolution, banners were on display in Kafranbel. Their slogans had a global echo because they touched on the most sensitive issues. Time and again, I had heard the name of one of the creators behind those slogans, but I had never met him before. When I headed for the north of Syria, our paths crossed, and it was the beginning of a new *pioneering*[6] commitment.

I entered Syria from Türkiye. I was keen to visit as many places as possible and to get a chance to film some material for my show, 'The Spirit of the Revolution'. Aleppo and its province, Hama's province, the coastal area, Idlib's province. Back then, the city of Idlib had not been liberated by the rebels yet. I wanted to shoot in all possible locations, because each episode of the show was about something different, which meant that I needed some outdoors footage. And obviously, since Kafranbel had been involved since the very early demonstrations, I thought it would be well worth my while to pay it a visit. Same as I had done previously in the areas around Hama and Idlib, I went there with the intention of staying for two days. Plus, I knew its *knight*[7] from his Facebook account, but since I had never met him before, this was the perfect chance to get to know him in person.

'The fault is within us, it's the Assad within each one of us, our victory
lies here: *until they change themselves. —Holy Quran, 13.11*'

Revolutionary Forces Rally in Kafranbel

19 April 2013

'Does Arab pride still exist? We turn to all Arabs and their conscience, not
to complain but to remind them. We may as well do them this favour'.

Revolutionary Forces Rally in Kafranbel

3 May 2013

'Resist, al-Qusayr... the road to the palace just got shorter'.

The Syrian Revolution in Kafranbel

20 May 2013

'We shall bury the sectarian match that you and that turbaned bigmouth
ally of yours keep striking... in al-Qusayr the nation shall come to life'.

The Syrian Revolution in Kafranbel

31 May 2013

Kafranbel anti-war banner. Unknown photographer, Khaled al-'Issa kneeling on left.

His name was Ra'ed al-Fares, and with him I visited the media office in Kafranbel for the first time. A wide one-storey building surrounded by plants and flowers with a thick door of steel. It took me a while to get in, as I was taking off my shoes, until one of the guys there said, 'Come on, jackass, hurry up'. I had seen that guy before, but I didn't know his name. I looked at him, and I thought it was strange that he called me that! He laughed, and his laughter made an impact on me. Again, he went, 'Come on in, hurry up'. I realised that it was just his sense of humour. His name was Khaled al-'Issa, and that's how he initiated a fond friendship that was going to lighten my burden for a while to come.

It took me only a couple of days to become friends with the rest of the guys there and for the media centre – which consisted of two large rooms, a small kitchen and a restroom – to occupy a special place in my heart. Kafranbel seemed to have migrated from Homs, carrying its spirit and settling anew in the Idlib province. The members of the media centre occupied the main room: Ra'ed, Khaled and Hamoud, and later on Abdallah, the soft-hearted revolutionary known as The Crocodile. They were all very kind people, and thanks to their cheerful disposition I spent a great time there. I made the closest bond with Ra'ed, though. There was an evident age gap between us, which made him a friend, a father, a pal, and a guide at the same time. The flower of the Revolution grew in his heart, as he had grown up in Kafranbel, south of Idlib. He had studied medicine, but he interrupted his studies and moved to Lebanon to start a new job, until he returned to Kafranbel in the 1990s, where he settled down and supported his wife and children working in real estate as well as being a contractual mediator.

It felt like we had known each other forever, and after all, our hearts had come close as they beat with the same revolutionary ardour. He organised peaceful demonstrations together with a group of young guys from his city back when the regime still had the cities of Idlib's province as well as a police station in the heart of the city under its control. This meant that Ra'ed, Hamoud, Khaled and Abdallah had to gradually leave Kafranbel. They moved to Jabala and some other villages in that area where they were safely away from regime control. There, they were able to organise demonstrations and take care of the logistics without distractions and intimidations. That would no longer be necessary after late 2012, as the regime lost its grip on Kafranbel, which then came under the spotlight and received international attention for its bilingual Arabic/English anti-regime slogans. Could it have been any different, since Ra'ed was behind them?

Like everybody else in the civil society movement, I always looked forward to the new Kafranbel slogans and to sharing them. I was blown away by the creativity, the sharp awareness of their message and by the irony. Every time the needle of our compass was shaking, Kafranbel made us laugh the whole matter off, despite all the grief.

They were great at teamwork. They were capable of mobilising young guys, galvanising the morale, and demonstrating discipline and dedication. They were all different in their own peculiar way. Ra'ed, for example, was the head of Radio Fresh, but he was also responsible for the Mazaya Women's Centre and its offices, for the centres offering psychological support to children, the training centre and the health services, all of which he had unified under one single umbrella organisation called the Union of Revolutionary Bureaus. This way he unreservedly brought the civil society aspect of the Revolution to the forefront. Obviously, this is what caused him to be subjected to an attempted murder by Islamic State militants, resulting in a serious wound in his chest, which only deepened his belief and firm conviction in the Revolution's trajectory.

Spending a great deal of time with him, I also found out about chances he had sacrificed, opportunities which would have allowed him to live well-off and to have long-term financial stability. Except, he never would've swapped his life in Kafranbel and his pursuit of country, freedom and Revolution for another city or a job.

✧ ✧ ✧

The more I spent time in Kafranbel, the more I enjoyed it. The more I got to know the guys in the media team, the more it became apparent how we were on the same wavelength. I decided to stay until the end of the week, but a week became two, three... our conversations were endless, their cheerful spirit made me forget the severity of the situation and dismiss the idea of going back to Türkiye.

I resumed doing civil society work and took part in demonstrations. When it became apparent that I was going to stay, the guys gave me a room and I settled in with them. With time, I became good friends with Khaled especially, since Ra'ed's medical condition didn't allow him to accompany me all the time when covering events. The battles of Wadi al-Dayef and al-Hamidiyyeh in the north broke out, and Ra'ed suggested that Khaled become my assistant. And obviously, being at the same time a leader and a friend, Ra'ed's recommendations were incontestable.

Over time, an image crystallised: Khaled and I became inseparable. He followed me during the day everywhere behind the camera as I stood in front of it, and when we set work aside, he was my loyal companion and fond friend when the night's darkness fell. Life was sweeter with him in it, despite all the bitterness, and the flame of the revolution only burned brighter, as if to say to Tarad: Don't be afraid, the blood of the martyrs was not shed in vain.

Apart from the work we did together, we would also go out together to relax, visit friends, eat, and cover the ongoing fighting. We witnessed the liberation of Idlib, the liberation of Ariha, the liberation of the Mastouma area with its checkpoints and military bases. We would wake up very early and spend long days documenting massacres. We would run together from alley to alley, from square to square, from one field hospital to another. He stood holding the camera, being my eyes, and I stood before him, being his voice, sometimes hoarse, sometimes breathless, sometimes accompanied by a tear. We were always trying to convey the suffering of the civilians. We stood in front of the rubble and told the world: these images are real. They may be too painful for fragile hearts to bear. Beneath the ruins, people lay whose bodies could no longer move, but whose spirits still burned.

The rasp of his voice was captivating, as was his smile, that had all the pride of a defiant youth. He had the ardour of the young revolutionary, he had quit secondary school to catch the revolutionary convoy and enroll at the school of freedom and homeland. He was imbued with revolutionary passion and went out of his way to cheer up his friends as though he himself were the cure for their troubles. And like all the revolution's children, he bore the mark of a bullet that stuck in his shoulder from one of the early peaceful demonstrations.

As for Hamoud, his story began very early in the revolution. His fingerprints were left on the walls in the form of anti-Assad slogans even before any organised movement began. He held a deep conviction in the cause of freedom and quickly emerged as a leader within the protest movement. A philosopher with a lust for life, that's what he was. He had the capacity to cheer us up with his wit and imagination that could put blood-stained dictators in an imaginary screenplay:

int., table – lunch: Assad is meeting with rebel leaders to congratulate them on their infighting and on the fragmentation of revolutionary forces instead of coming together against him!

Although he was the best at bringing back memories with his camera, he was also a member of the White Helmets. He provided first aid to those whose lives he couldn't save with his camera, and he was a pragmatist. He witnessed the bloodshed in his beloved hometown, but he tirelessly hoped he could continue saving people.

Ra'ed's face, Hamoud's voice, Khaled's laughter, this whole panorama coalesced into a clear idea: Kafranbel is the Revolution's epitome.

A Long Nightmare

Life, after all, is like that. It's this and that, the sweet and the sour. Our smiles lightened our sorrows when the night's black curtains were lowered at the end of the day. Friendship had the capacity to magically relieve our burdens. We laughed a lot, and the distance from our loved ones was the main enemy on our uneven path. We had to stick together and keep shouting as one voice that ripped apart the homeland's sky first and that of the digital world next. If one of us got hurt, all of us felt the pain so as to speed up his recovery. Neither words nor pages nor anecdotes can convey what this friendship meant to us.

I was in Türkiye for work that day. Khaled rang me and told me Ra'ed and Hamoud were missing. They had headed over to Saraqib, but they had been incommunicado, which meant that they were probably in the outskirts of Kafranbel, or in Ma'arrat al-Nu'man if not in Saraqib. We waited for a whole day, the wait felt longer and longer as time passed, it felt even longer because of the long distance. Waiting for someone is tough enough but waiting for someone when you can't contact them is even harder. We heard nothing about them. I started taking guesses – they'd been kidnapped or killed. I prayed to God that they were not being tortured following an arrest… I was still hurting from Tarad's departure. I cried even at the remote possibility of death or abuse. I said, 'It's my luck, and I know it! Ra'ed's journey must have come to a close in Saraqib, I'll never have any friends again. I won't find another incarnation of the Revolution like him, all is lost'.

Early the next day, I called Khaled hoping for good news, but he had nothing. The whole situation was even tougher for me under a Turkish sky whose shade of blue wasn't that of my homeland, no matter how similar. I was so upset and confused that I held my face in my hands and decided to go back to Syria. Maybe they'll magically come back, I thought. I booked a plane ticket from Istanbul to Hatay, a city located near the Syria-Türkiye border. Our flight almost got cancelled because of a storm, but they then decided to just delay it a few hours. I was ready to walk from Istanbul to Syria in case the plane broke down. I started talking to myself: I can't stay here twiddling my thumbs. After a long and excruciating wait, the good news came, and I felt relieved – the flight was not cancelled. We boarded the plane, but we stayed on the runway for ages before it took off, to the extent that I thought it was never going to leave. Shortly after that, the plane ran into some turbulence and instructions for evacuation were circulated to the terrified passengers. Lights pointing in the direction of the emergency exit were switched on, and the captain addressed the passengers in Turkish. Many of us lost our composure and screamed until the members of the cabin crew intervened to calm the waters. Despite the bad weather and this rollercoaster ride of feelings and thoughts, the plane eventually landed in Hatay, where a friend picked me up and drove me to the border crossing. Khaled and his friend Ali were expecting me on the other side of the border. When I got there at 5:30 p.m., the crossing was closed, so to speed things up a little I had no other choice but to call upon someone I knew there, a Turkish person, to let me go through as an exception, on account of the extraordinary situation I was in. I crossed into Syria and found my friends waiting for me. They told me they had information about Ra'ed's whereabouts. He was being detained by Jabhat al-Nusra in Ma'arrat al-Nu'man, which narrowed down the search area and saved us a lot of trouble.

We drove through a thick fog from Bab al-Hawa to Ma'arrat al-Nu'man but thankfully didn't crash into any cars. We arrived in Ma'arrat al-Nu'man at 8 p.m., but we still needed to locate Jabhat al-Nusra's prison where Ra'ed and Hamoud were being detained. We drove from one Jabhat al-Nusra office to another until we came across Ra'ed's car parked outside one of the buildings. I immediately went in to ask about them. I introduced myself, and the people there greeted me.

'My friends are being detained by you'.

'Who are your friends'?

'Ra'ed Fares and Hamoud Junayd – I want to see them'.

They made me wait a little, then one of their security officers emerged and informed me that they only had Hamoud. I understood immediately that they weren't interested in Hamoud, they wanted Ra'ed because they'd been looking for him for a while.

'No way, it's either both of them or neither'.

Eventually they admitted that they had Ra'ed too, but his name was not registered there because, to my anger, they were going to transfer him to the Harim prison, which was also under Jabhat al-Nusra's control and where he would very likely be executed. I snarled at them to let both of them go and kept badgering them with questions about the accusations that had been levelled against my friends.

They came up with some fabrications about Ra'ed and Hamoud being agents of the regime. I told them I lived with these guys, and if that were true, then I would be too. Then when they said that Ra'ed hated Islam, I showed them a picture of him praying *Jum'ah* with us, refuting their accusation.

They stopped eventually. You convinced us, they said, but the decision needs to be approved by a judge! Every time I won an argument with someone, they declined responsibility for the matter and dumped it onto someone else above them. I felt like I was going around in circles.

When the judge finally showed up at last, he agreed to Hamoud's immediate release and Ra'ed's two days later. That didn't give me any sense of relief though, because they were probably lying, especially since Ra'ed's name was not registered there. I didn't cave. I kept arguing with them at length. My hope was that they would be lenient and that things wouldn't go sour, so I threatened to launch a popular campaign against them and tried to use that as a bargaining chip in exchange for them letting my friends go free. They unwillingly let me and Khaled see Ra'ed, and they brought him out with two huge guys in balaclavas alongside him. I hugged him immediately and managed to whisper to him their preposterous accusations against him, but the two big guys pushed me away harshly and prevented me from talking to him. That reminded me of the tyranny of the regime.

'You're just like the Assad regime, like ISIS, like any other brutal regime in the world'.

'Don't compare us to those delinquents!'

'You're not in any way different of them! By God, I will expose you!'

The judge stepped in, trying to calm us down.

'I will confer with Ra'ed briefly and make a decision about his case'.

The judge agreed to his release on the condition that no mention of the events would be made in the media. This woeful display thankfully ended at 2 a.m. when we left the place. Ra'ed and Hamoud were coming home safe with us and nothing else mattered.

'To the Revolution and to the deadly rockets... to the shrapnel of the wandering night... to the pictures of the martyrs... and the cameras' lenses... to the full extent of our Revolution! I will open my wounds and live, my dearest friends, in the agony of your absence'.

We spent some lovely days in Kafranbel, despite all the oppression and the pain. Khaled, Ra'ed and Hamoud gave those days such a sweet and pleasant touch, it hurts even more to remember them. I entered a nice routine working on civil society projects with Ra'ed at the child support and social development centres, as well as another training centre for which I was personally responsible. One of the two halls there was named after Tarad, the other one after Ghiath Matar, may God have mercy on their souls. In addition, Khaled and I carried on our media coverage of the crimes perpetrated constantly by the Assad regime against civilians in the north of Syria. We went from village to village, from city to city. We worked so hard hoping that someone would listen. The Assad regime was no longer our only enemy – we considered all parties whose abuse against civilians we exposed as our enemies. Hezbollah, Iran, Iraqi militias, and ISIS.

Why, You Infidel!

January 2015

In the early months of 2015, one day I was having breakfast with Khaled, Ra'ed and Hamoud, when someone started banging on our door. They were pounding on it so adamantly that before we could even understand what was going on, the door came off its hinges and a guy wearing a balaclava appeared, carrying a rifle, barking at us, ordering us to raise our hands. It wasn't very long before we realised that the whole place was surrounded by armed men and heavy artillery such as KPV 14.5mm machine guns, as if it were a military base, as though the food on our table were a battlefield. This time we had no idea who they were or what they wanted. One of them was blocking the door, preventing us from seeing what was outside. Then a group of them attacked the radio station office adjacent to ours. We coordinated all our civil society activities in the other offices, and I knew that they would recognise me as soon as they saw me. I thought I'd use my reputation as leverage to make them stop this raid. They had by now spread everywhere – it was a horrible scene to witness, strikingly evocative of raids conducted by the regime's mukhabarat. I approached the guy standing by the door and told him that I wanted to go out. He said no. But out I went anyway and spoke to the guy in the balaclava.

'My name is Hadi Abdullah from Homs. Would you care to tell me who you guys are and what do you want exactly?'

He knocked me down and he barked at me, 'You guys are insulting the Prophet, you infidel!'

With whatever was left of my patience I rose and confronted his meaningless claim. I started hitting him, and he hit me back. A vocal altercation ensued, during which I shouted in his face, 'Who is your leader? Who's in charge of this operation?'

Khaled had been observing the whole thing, and he lost his temper when he saw them put their hands on me. In an attempt to save me, he went for the only gun we had in the office – a 7.5 calibre pistol – but before he could get near it, Ra'ed had calmed him down to make sure that we, the victims, didn't turn into the culprits. We found out from the guy in charge of the whole operation that they'd figured they were in the wrong place due to a miscommunication. By then, though, they had already wreaked enough havoc to terrify us. They claimed they ended up there by accident and that the raid was a big mistake; they thought they could get away with knocking our door down and leaving that mayhem behind by just apologising to us. We later found out that another armed group connected to them had raided the Mazaya Centre, which was under the leadership of Khaled's mother Ghaliah and belonged to the same revolutionary umbrella organisation that Ra'ed had put together. During their raid they also threatened the women, looted the centre, broke things and took everything they could put their hands on. All these attempts ultimately failed to weaken the grassroots movement. Quite the contrary, each raid resulted in more popular support on a broader scale.

In the Revolutionaries' Prison

September 2015

Every now and again, a hostile wind blew in our faces. Every time the skies cleared and the sun shone upon us, adverse events hit us like a storm making us face reality. War has a way of balancing the blows of the cold and the heat, of fear and hope, and death collects the souls of the young and the aged without distinction, burning its memory equally into the hearts of children and elderly.

One day, a physician from the city of Salamiyyeh near Hama, a woman who had given generously to the cause of the Revolution since its inception, called us to inform us that her two children and her mother had gone missing in Idlib. The were believed to be held by one of the rebel groups. She wanted me to step in to find them and intercede for their liberation. Ra'ed and I asked around and inquired until we found out that they were being detained in the Za'iniyyeh prison near Latakia. We headed over there straightaway, I introduced myself and they welcomed us. I told them I was looking for a family and that I wanted to know the accusations that had been levelled at them. I was told that the members of that family were wanted by the Assad regime and that one of the rebel groups had arrested them near the border as they were trying to make their way into Türkiye. I tried to win their sympathy, hoping that they would release the three, but they categorically refused. This being a moral cause that would attract a lot of support, I decided to fire the one weapon that could hurt the rebel group: pressure from the general public. I threatened them with mobilising people and after some negotiation they agreed to let me meet with the grandmother and her grandchildren. It was a horrible display. They were in dire straits. The situation of the prison was as deplorable as if they were being held by the regime, not a rebel group. This was not the first time a revolutionary organisation had committed such an error. They lost sight of the fact that justice against oppression in all its forms was their mission, not fighting against each other.

I first met with the grandmother. She was still in a state after having been subjected to torture. They wanted to use her as a bargaining chip and hand her to the regime in exchange for the liberation of some of the fighters' wives. The sheer idea was horrific. To trade an innocent in exchange for other innocents…! What's even worse is that the likely outlook for the grandmother was going to be either death under barbaric forms of torture or, best-case scenario, being executed straightaway.

I was strongly against this plan, and at the same time, I tried to keep her calm. I told her I was acting on behalf of her daughter the physician and her daughter's two children, which relieved her a little. It was a few minutes before they brought in the two kids, the eldest thirteen years old and rattling with fear, and her brother behind her. I told them that their uncle and their mother had sent me, and that I would never leave them. The eldest was reassured to hear her uncle's name and hugged me tight. Tears dropped from her and Ra'ed's eyes almost simultaneously. It was the first time I saw him crying. Unable to endure the whole scene, Ra'ed left the room, whereas I stayed, soothed and reassured them for the whole duration of our meeting.

I asked for them to be released, but my request was met with refusal. They claimed that the 'jail guard' had to approve the decision first.

'Okay', I said, 'where is he?'

'He's not here', they said.

'Let's go to his house', I said.

'It's late', they said. 'He's at the battlefront now, and you can't meet with him'.

These and other excuses meant that we had to wait until the next morning to meet with this guy. The prison was located a two hours' drive away from Kafranbel, so we set off at eight in the morning and got there at 10 a.m. Like the men we had met before him, at first he said no, then his attitude seemed to change when I mentioned the possibility of a public campaign, but eventually he left the matter in the hands of their commander in Latakia. Without the commander's approval – he claimed – he was not in a position to settle such a matter. Naturally, when we asked about the commander's whereabouts, they told us he was travelling abroad and that we wouldn't be able to see him. We didn't know what to do but we insisted, and they referred us to the commander's deputy, except we had to wait until the next day to meet him.

The sun rose to yet another day in detention for the family whose hearts were dying to be reunited. Ra'ed and I headed over to the prison to meet with the grandmother and her two grandchildren, but the guards wouldn't let us see them again. The only alternative we had was to go talk to the deputy commander. We explained to him that the matter was now in his hands and that we were hoping he would pardon them and let them go, but I lost my temper and snarled at him. I told him again that I thought they were as evil as the Assad regime. He didn't appreciate that; in fact, he got very upset and told me not to compare the two. By now, anything either of us said made the other flare up, and eventually he decreed that the family was never going to leave.

We headed over to the Bab al-Hawa area to meet with the commander general, but it wasn't easy to get hold of him. We persevered and eventually managed to meet with several commanders. I insisted with them that I was never going to give up on this family until they agreed to release them. I also warned them that they were leaving me no choice but to launch a media campaign against them. Eventually they agreed with me about this family's rights, but they explained to me that the 'Latakia Division' opposed the idea of releasing the family and that they were keen to avoid any disagreements with them. We managed to convince them to move the grandmother and the two children to the Bab al-Hawa prison, where a judge would decide on their release. This meant that they had to spend yet another day in detention, unable to enjoy freedom. Once they had been transferred to Bab al-Hawa, we spent the whole day swaying between seeing the judge and waiting for him, as he kept postponing and delaying the decision until the clock struck 10 p.m. Ra'ed and I could not move around easily because of the tight security, but they allowed us to meet with the grandmother and the two children. We kept them company and reassured them that the wheels were in motion and that they would be released anytime now. Then I rang their uncle so they could talk and assuage each other's fears. We decided that Ra'ed would leave, whereas I would stay in the prison with the grandmother and the two children. I instructed Ra'ed to post a message on social media platforms saying that for the first time Hadi Abdullah had to spend a night in confinement in what was, sadly, a rebel-controlled prison. That was it, we had no other choice. Putting his own life at risk at a time when multiple groups were looking to get their hands on him, Ra'ed set off alone in the middle of the night, leaving me with the three detainees. An hour later I was still arguing with some of the military leaders when I bumped into the commander general, who waived away the whole matter as a misunderstanding. The two children and their grandmother were free to go! I called Ra'ed immediately. I asked him not to post anything on social media, come back and drive us all home. We took the grandmother and the two children to our media centre, where they had a chance to shower up and put on clean clothes, which Khaled's mother kindly provided.

Here was the bright side of the Revolution, healing the wounds that the Revolution itself had caused. Gradually, the family's feelings towards the Revolution changed and transitioned from regret to a renewed sense of pride. The revolutionary cause was something worth being displaced for. Throughout their stay with us they got to know Khaled and his mother and learned about our media activism. We then helped them make their way into Türkiye, where they reunited with their loved ones.

Confiscated: Restraining Order

I couldn't sleep a wink until five in the morning that night. The huge amount of work that had piled up meant staying up until late, and when I did manage to put my head down and sleep, it was only for an hour and a half. That was when Khaled came and woke me up at half past six in the morning. I was still exhausted, but I couldn't stay in bed after he told me, 'Get up, get up, get up! The place is full of fighters...' By the time I had rolled out of bed and stretched my tired limbs, the whole place was surrounded. I went down and found the fighters eagerly taking anything they could put their hands on and transferring it to their vehicles. They started with our radio equipment, then moved on to the other offices. They went into my room and took the cameras and the laptops. One of them even took the cooling fans, although it was winter. I looked at him and I laughed as I remarked, 'Nicely done, at least you're taking something useful!' He stared at me with a frown then carried on with his task. The worst was when one of them took Tarad's camera. I raised my voice and said, 'Take everything but not this one, this is very dear to me...' They took it all the same and told me I might be able to retrieve it later once they had stored the booty in their facilities. That camera was a keepsake – it contained Tarad's last shots that he took right before he died. They were brutal in the way they handled it. I felt like they were stabbing me in the heart.

The looting lasted for approximately two hours, and all the while we were not free to leave the place. Then they let everyone else go except me and Ra'ed. They grabbed him and put something on his eyes. They wanted to take him away with them, but I stood in the way and insisted, 'You will have to take us both'. I knew they held a grudge against Ra'ed – I couldn't let him go alone with them. They knew about my media activism and eventually they allowed me to accompany Ra'ed. Shortly before we left the centre, they went in again and wrote:

'X X CONFISCATED BY JABHAT AL-NUSRA: NO TRESPASSING X X'

They drove Ra'ed to the infamous 'Uqab prison. They took me to one of their houses where I was so scared for Ra'ed I thought I would die of fear and of sadness over Tarad's beloved camera. I felt my hands were tied and unable to do anything to help Ra'ed, neither to retrieve what they had taken. I couldn't even do anything for myself. That's it, I whispered to myself, they're going to kill him, my second personal tragedy after Tarad's departure.

Khaled was not with us. He stayed at the centre and witnessed the looting, then managed to talk them into letting him in again, claiming he forgot his house keys inside. He went in to find out that they had looted the fridge too. They ate all the food in it, and they would probably have taken it had they managed to carry it. They trashed my room. Khaled stealthily shot some pictures and videos of the place, then sneaked out and proceeded to circulate them on social media alongside a post in which he denounced the whole thing and demanded public support. According to everyone on social media platforms such as Facebook and Twitter, as well as international media networks, Ra'ed and Hadi had been arrested. Local and national demonstrations were under preparation, and I couldn't have been happier. Pressure mounted on Jabhat al-Nusra until they became fearful of an attack against them and had no other choice but to send an envoy to solve the issue. We sat down to talk with him, and I laid out my conditions. There were two Tunisian men with him who listened to the whole conversation. I talked to each one of them individually until we reached an agreement according to which Ra'ed and I were to be released and Jabhat al-Nusra was to return all the stolen equipment – this was the first time Jabhat al-Nusra returned anything they took. In return for that, we would circulate an article providing an account of the events in which we mentioned that Ra'ed had done something wrong. He didn't do anything wrong – we were forced to write that – but this was all we were ready to compromise on in order to cut this deal.

Much as this was a significant moral compromise, I was over the moon when they finally released Ra'ed. I am not going to lose another Tarad, I said to myself. They allowed me to pick him up and take him to his freedom. I drove my car and followed them to one of their checkpoints on the outskirts of Kafranbel. There they instructed me to stop, to prevent me from looking inside the prison, and wait for Ra'ed to arrive.

The prison door opened and a guard in a balaclava shouted Ra'ed Fares's name. When Ra'ed inquired about the place to which they were taking him the guard barked, 'Walk and keep your mouth shut. Are you the media guy?'

'Yes', said Ra'ed, 'I'm the media guy'.

'What do you do for a living?'

'Media stuff, what do you think?'

'Yeah, keep walking, smarten up'.

They took him by the hands, and they put something black over his eyes, like a fabric bag, then they put him into a van. Ra'ed thought they were going to kill him. He was sure. That sentence, 'Keep walking, smarten up', the fact that he worked in media, and that bag on his head were all evidence indicating only one thing: death. The road seemed to him to be very long. They drove on both paved and dirt roads. Thousands of thoughts crossed his mind on the way to his death. Perhaps he thought about the ones he loved and how they would take the news, but the best news came when they pulled the bag from his head and ordered him to get out of the car. He saw me smiling at him, I ran in his direction, hugged him and thanked God that he was fine and healthy. I never thought I would see him in good shape again.

As I drove him to his family's house, all the while I told him about the negotiations and the agreement we had reached, as well as the anguish I experienced in his absence. Everyone was waiting for him at the house, and as soon as we walked in, his elderly mother could not fight back the tears. She hugged him, and then she hugged me. I was like a son to her, she said.

As per our agreement, I did write the article, but we couldn't agree on a final draft. I mentioned that they had stomped on the Revolution's flag; they didn't want me to write about that. They tried to get rid of several passages in the article, but I didn't accept it. I told them I would mention that Ra'ed had done something wrong, but I had no intention of providing a false account of the events. On the same bright sunny day the article came out, they let us go and returned the equipment.

Hadi the Martyr

7 October 2015

As though one oppressor was not enough, the Russian air force entered the battlefield, vigorously, eager to join the other global bloodthirsty regimes that the Revolution faced. In the early days of the Russian invasion, Khaled, Hamoud and I covered the ongoing fighting. Back then the siege of Hama was at its peak and the 'tanks massacre'[8] had just happened.

I had been filming the clashes between the Russians and the Free Syrian Army, when a fake page carrying my name, Hadi Abdullah, shared the news of my death through someone's fake personal profile. People bought it and circulated the information on social media, oblivious to the fact that this played right into the regime's hands. Many people tried to get in touch with us, but we were incommunicado in an area with no signal until the late evening, by which time Hamoud and Khaled had already received confirmation from one of my friends that I was supposedly dead.

As I was driving back from filming the incinerated tanks and the rebels' response to the Russian intervention, a family stopped us on the road and asked us whether we had been to the battle front and was it true that Hadi Abdullah was actually dead? ... I was obviously dumbfounded. I laughed and told them who I was, Hadi himself. They invited me to come out of the car, kissed me and thanked God profusely that I was still alive. We found out from them that social media pages and news networks had been spreading fake news of my assassination.

Then a rebel checkpoint stopped us, and as soon as one of the officers recognised me, he was stunned and invoked God because he also thought I was dead. That made me realise the extent to which the news had spread. When we got to the media centre, Ra'ed wasn't there, he was out inquiring and asking around about us. He headed back when he lost hope and found us waiting for him. He was so happy he couldn't contain himself – he started hitting us amicably and reproachfully, still frightened for us. He hugged one of us with one hand and hit someone else with the other. He looked like he didn't know whether to be happy that we were back or angry because we disappeared!

Khaled teased him, 'Wow we were better off dead than with your reprimands!' ...

'Indeed', Ra'ed said, 'I really should give you a beating, I didn't realise how dear you were to me, I didn't know life was meaningless without you guys'.

I then sat down with my mobile phone and found hundreds of messages and missed calls from my friends and family. I called my family first, and their tears almost made me cry too. I told them everything and promised it would never happen again. 'Tell me soft words, even if they're lies', as the poet said.

#Aleppo_is_burning

Khaled and I worked full time on media coverage. There seemed to be a unity of intent behind the non-stop bombing to punish ordinary people. While we were busy trying to document what was happening in and around Idlib, a coordinated Russian-Iranian campaign began in Aleppo to support the regime in its attempt to wipe out the local population there. We had no choice but to move to Aleppo into a flat located in the al-Shi'ar area of the city, not very far from the Bayan hospital and close to an organisation called *Inqaz* which provided first-aid assistance. That was the best location for us to be able to set off with the ambulances and reach the site of the incidents, despite this being a dangerous breach of security regulations.

Massacres took place every day without exceptions, and we slogged away to take shots and keep account of victims and wounded. It was a two-colour picture: grey with some red in it. Death became normalised, and there was not a glimpse of hope on the horizon. However, citizen journalism played a key role in the launching of the #Aleppo_is_burning campaign on social media in an attempt to stop the bombing through pressure from the general public. And indeed, the campaign landed a three-week truce which gave us some time to go back to Kafranbel. Three weeks later we were back to where we had started, running from one area of Aleppo to the other, capturing with our camera whatever was left.

✦ ✦ ✦

Then Ramadan came. As we had always done before, Khaled and I remained committed to fasting despite the heat and the ongoing war, both of which would have been morally acceptable reasons to exempt us. We woke up around 7 a.m. to the sound of airplanes which announced the beginning of the massacres and with them, work. Since it was Ramadan, a month during which people tend to sleep longer, normally we would start live streaming at a time while our viewers were still asleep. We ran tirelessly behind every barrel bomb to film those bloody faces as they cried for help, hoping their voices would reach someone's conscience. Khaled was always very supportive, particularly when the lack of response made me lose motivation, and he reminded me how long and tough the road to freedom is.

Through our walkie talkies we learned about massacres taking place. One day we heard about one that had just happened in the Jisr al-Hajj neighbourhood in Aleppo. We picked up our equipment and drove as fast as we could. We started shooting as soon as we got there. Except for minor details, we were looking at the usual: debris, blood, bodies. Before the smoke had even lifted, the other guys at the scene were warning us about the likelihood of another airstrike on the very same place. The planes had not left yet. No sooner had we positioned ourselves a few metres away from the site of the airstrike than barrel bombs and rockets rained on the very same spot causing more destruction, as though one strike alone would not have been sufficient. I say 'barrel bombs rained' as though describing a scene from a violent cartoon for kids: a scene with black smoke and fog before the screams broke the silence following the explosion. That's if there were anyone lucky enough to have survived.

'Military aviation continues to target civilian houses and markets. A few minutes ago, it blasted these markets with four rockets, which resulted in massive destruction and fires, as you can see. The White Helmets are doing

what they can to put out the fires and extract the bodies of the martyrs and the injured. We see here tens of martyrs and injured, while Syrians await humanitarian aid, airplanes hit markets, cars are bombed, shops are closed down, people are targeted while they're shopping for essentials... airplanes have become a common sight'.

I say 'victims' as though I were counting things I bought from some shop. I say 'injured' as though they were dolls. You get used to it; dull colours become normality.

As I call out again, trying to hopelessly make my voice heard, I repeat myself,

'Another entire neighbourhood has been hit by a rocket. There are no words to describe the extent of the destruction and of the people's distress... shouldn't the victims' remains deserve a new and adequate language to express the extent of the tragedy? Even the dead are blasted in their graves... no one, not even the dead and the animals, escapes the bombing'.

We were back filming when six barrel bombs came down on us. Khaled was still in the car getting the cameras ready, I had already started filming. War doesn't leave anyone any time to wonder why someone survived while someone else got hit. It marks everyone's body with wounds, and it scars everyone's soul. One of these barrel bombs landed some ten metres away from us. It was a few minutes until the smoke turned into rubble and a voice exclaimed 'Allahu akbar'. The camera in my hand quivered... it had been filming since the beginning, preserving for history the images of light poles drowned in smoke, of people's 'Allahu akbar' rising through that same smoke as they ran to help the victims. 'Allahu akbar', a collapsed wall and its debris on the ground. 'Allahu akbar', a building oscillating, trying not to fall and make things worse. 'Allahu akbar', a suffocating tree. 'Allahu akbar', a sky in the throes of death, a choking throat, an ascending soul.

'Allahu akbar', 'Allahu akbar'.

The Unbreakable Pledge

The screen turned upside down. Rocks and debris. My whole field of vision now nothing but dust. 'Khaled!' I shouted, 'I got hit in the head!' I was still filming when my life flashed before my eyes. The image became blurry and started resembling what every reporter experiences in the deaths of others, those last moments captured by the camera. As I opened my eyes my main concern was to make sure the camera had been filming... then I heard someone call my name... the screen was shaken as the names 'Hadi' and 'Khaled' blended with the smoke. Khaled came and took the camera as per our agreement: that each one of us would take up filming in case the other got hurt. My head felt heavy on its left side – instinctively I lifted my hand to prop it up, and I sensed the stream of warm blood running through my fingers. Somebody lifted me up and took me to an ambulance. The image moved alongside us on the pavement, as if trying to run faster than the next barrel bomb. The images spoke louder than words. Feet rushing, a door opening, the screen is shaken again, the word PRESS written on a vest that didn't stop the injuries, a hand on a bleeding scar, the lens of a driver's mobile phone filming with one hand and holding the steering wheel of an ambulance with his other hand. Again, written in red a sentence that would make the people watching laugh later: 'Fasten your seat belt'. Khaled's angelic face and his blond hair spattered with blood, his facial features on the verge of melting in excruciating pain, the sound of an ambulance which we never thought someone would have to call for us.

Yet another scene. I kept asking him 'Are you okay, Khaled? Are you alright?' A tragic sight, the hospital floor covered in unknown people's blood. The camera looks up a little, the radiator on the lower part of the wall and above it some shelves with bags and boxed medical supplies. I take off my bulletproof press vest, take a look at Khaled to make sure he's okay, I touch my head, but I feel the blood pouring out from my forehead. I open the tap and splash water on my face to wash away the blood. Perhaps that might relieve the pain. The doctor's hands move up and down as they stitch the wound on my head. Khaled was laid on a stretcher with a smile on his face, flashing the victory sign with his fingers up in the air.

Those barrel bombs would have easily wiped out an entire building, and we only had God to thank for making it out of there alive. Khaled caught some shrapnel while he was still in the car, whereas I took cover behind an earthen barricade, but same as my mate, I also caught some shrapnel, which cost me five stitches. We were bleeding copiously; therefore, we had to interrupt the fasting and made our way back to our place.

I told him the same thing over and over every day, 'Khaled *habibi*, watch out, we came very close to dying today... I can't stand losing you. We die together or we live together'. He knew how much I loved him and how much the idea of losing him frightened me. He loved me as much as I loved him, perhaps more, and he never refused me a request. He was not allowed to go into a dangerous place before me – he wasn't allowed to go anywhere I hadn't set foot. I tried always to stay as close to him as possible so that death wouldn't miss one or the other. I said to him, 'Should anything happen to you, I'd kill myself. I'd commit suicide'. He laughed, but this time he also couldn't figure why I wanted to impress him. I was trying to scare and dissuade him from dying, as though it were his decision when his time came. I repeated, 'I will kill myself if anything happens to you. I will jump from on top of the Bayan hospital…' I knew that my disappointment was his point of weakness, so imagine when I threatened him with jumping from the tallest building in Aleppo… I didn't want the same person that could keep a smile on amidst the devastation caused by a rocket to disappear in its smoke.

He turned serious. The gleam of his look suddenly scared me, and he sounded rattled. 'Why are you saying this to me now?' he said. 'I'll never forgive you'. Then he continued, 'Let's just promise each other that if one of us dies, the other one'll carry on'.

I shook my head, 'No way' I said, '… you don't fool me, I don't want to promise anything… how am I going to be able to continue without you?' It might be possible for someone to still see with one eye only, but how can I in God's holy name see with my eyes shut? When I noticed that he was receptive to my idea I became more lenient… 'Let's make a pledge', I said. Little did I know about how costly this pledge was going to be, nor that that would be our last night together. And as if Tarad's memory weren't enough to keep me up at night, that conversation too put another bell that tolls in my ear.

The next day, bandages on our heads, we went out to work. In the evening, we headed over to the hospitals to have our wounds cleaned and the bandages removed by the doctors. The siege brought us close to the doctors, so we spent the first hours of the night at their place conversing amicably. Around 11 p.m. we took the last picture together and made our way back to our place.

I will never forget the scene. Aleppo's bullet-riddled buildings, with their narrow entrances by the alleyways. I was driving us home. I parked near our building's main entrance. Our flat was on the third floor. We were staying in Aleppo's al-Shi'ar area. I started going up the stairs first while Khaled was talking to one of the neighbors. As I had always warned him not to walk in before me, I went first, although the building was supposedly safe.

Under the Debris

17 June 2016

The last thing I remember, he was five or six metres behind me, when suddenly I felt water flowing under my feet shortly before I got electrocuted. I didn't know where the electricity came from... for a moment I thought it came from the electricity meter that was located above the front door, or perhaps from the water meter... Wait a second, though... why am I covered in debris consisting of rocks and iron? I asked myself this even though I could barely breathe. While still getting electrocuted, I noticed something else had happened: my entire body was buried under rubble, and I was unable to move. I realised, though, that before I could settle into a comfortable position, someone had to switch off the source of the power current. I thought, let me ask Khaled to do that... he couldn't possibly have been under the rubble too because he was a few metres behind me... I could barely utter anything when I called him, 'Khaled, man, can you hear me? I'm here, tell them to switch the power off'.

It was a few minutes before I realised what had happened. An explosion caused the building to collapse on top of me, the electric cables came down with it and stuck to my body causing the attrition... Then to make things worse, the water pipes blew up. For more than ten minutes the pain was excruciating and unbearable. There was nothing I could do, and I just surrendered to it. My hands were stuck under a collapsed wall, and I couldn't move my feet at all. The roof lay firm on my chest. I waited for so long I thought I was dead. I groaned, although I was barely able to whisper, begging for someone to turn the power off, until I had no discernible reason even to be alive.

In a situation like that, even thinking is a challenge. As destiny would have it, the only way to breathe was a tiny little hole through which I called my dear friend, 'Khaled, man, tell them to switch the power off...' Then I compromised, I cut the second part of the sentence, my only hope was that I could hear something, even if it were just a whisper. 'Khaled!'

I lost hope that he would ever hear me, but I kept groaning: 'Hey! Anybody out there, can you hear me? Please turn the power off, I beg of you!' ... The truth is, in a situation like that, your heart beats to the rhythm of 'Yaa Marhaba bil-mawt'.⁹ I started recalling all the times I'd been close to death before... the day a bullet missed me... all the times a place we'd just been to got bombed... the barrel bombs that left scars on us two days before... Under the debris, I was convinced that I was as close to it as I'd ever come. I won't lie, I was happy. With all the pain I was in, I felt I was being eased of my responsibilities – from now on, no more causes to fight for. Having fought for a cause myself, I would become a martyr and then someone else would pick up where I left off... I thought about martyrdom and that God the Almighty might not accept me as a martyr, so I sought his forgiveness for all the sins that I might have committed. I uttered the two shahadas, the way someone who's about to die would do. I remembered my family, my dad and my mother... my siblings... Ra'ed... these people, the people I love... then Khaled's vision came back, wiped off everything else and he was all I thought about. How will he live without me... will he keep his promise? Will God forgive me? I was still in pain; in the last moments of my life, I heard Khaled's voice through the rubble.

Let's say I heard a voice similar to Khaled's... Or maybe I just heard whatever I wanted to hear, even if it wasn't really him.

Although I had completely surrendered to death, I felt relieved when

I heard his voice, like seeing the light at the end of a tunnel. The intensity of the electric shocks decreased even though I was still getting electrocuted. Khaled – or someone else who sounded like him – asked me where I was and told me they'd turned the power off, but they also told me that there was still one active cable. I asked them to cut that too and when they did, I was able to unbend... the electric shocks stopped at last... The pain gradually faded, like salt slowly dissolving in a glass of water. All I needed now was to pass out and wait until they extracted whatever was left of my body to carry on with my life. I asked God to make me fall asleep or lose consciousness to be able to get some rest. I lost the sense of time, I have no idea how long I was there for, how much thinking I did, how much I groaned, how long I waited at one time for both death and survival. The clock's hands stop when you're stuck like that, and you go back and forth between what has been and what will be. You have no other choice but to wait: will I stay like this? And if not, what will happen to me?

I woke up again, regaining consciousness after God knows how long. When I came to my senses something was digging above me, and I heard that very familiar sound: the White Helmets' excavator. It dug and dug. Its buzzing sound mixed with the voices of several people filled my ears. Suddenly the roles were reversed – the same excavator that I had time and again filmed saving people was now forcing its way through the wreckage for me; the same voices that I had tried to convey so many times were silenced, and God decreed that I be buried here and needed someone to convey my own voice. War was quick to make me transition from reporter to the subject of a report, to mute those voices with an explosion, so deafeningly loud I didn't even hear it.

It was a few minutes before my hope that the excavator would make me come out alive turned into yet another concern: what if they keep digging but miss me? What if they miscalculate the depth of the rubble and dig through my flesh? But I was in too much pain... I didn't have the energy to think about the possibility of being stabbed by a digger, on top of the pain I was already enduring... not a single inch of my body would have been able to bear more. I found comfort in the fact that in all the excavations for bodies that I had been a witness to, I'd never seen one in which the rescuers mistakenly hurt the people under the rubble. And yet, what if I was the first one?

I slowly emerged from under the wreckage – first they removed the rocks from my legs, then I was able to feel my belly and my chest. My head was still stuck between iron or cement, I'm not sure which... it took a few more groans from me and a little more twisting from them to pull it out. I was literally covered with blood, my eyes were so bruised, and I was so riddled with wounds I was unrecognisable. My body was broken, my head was jam-packed with thoughts and my tongue wouldn't stop asking about Khaled.

The place was noisy and looked mostly very grim except for the light coming from the rescuers' helmets. When I saw the video titled, 'The moment Hadi Abdallah is rescued from under the rubble – may God restore his health soon', I felt like I shot the video myself. As though that buried body wasn't Hadi's, as if those people that gathered around me were talking to someone else, as if they made all that noise to make sure they saved yet another one of us from being a number on the list of martyrs... as if the whole world wouldn't so much as look at them, anyway.

A bunch of people gather in a circle, some trying to pull him out, some to check on him, some to document the event. Some place his bloody, wretched body on a stretcher and rush him to the ambulance. Every word or sentence is repeated two or three times for emphasis: shoot, shoot! Get away, get away! Get your hands off him, get your hands off him! Shut the door, shut the door! Before he knows it, he's inside the ambulance. They close the door and dash down the road until they disappear.

My Other Eye

Despite the fog that blocked my vision, it was a familiar sight... I tried to open my eyes while my eyelids instinctively struggled to shut the image out completely. I looked up and down, but I couldn't see Khaled, and I badly wanted reassuring news about him. But instead of his features, which would've been enough to ease my pain no matter how excruciating it was, all I could see was the doctor's face, the same one who changed my bandages the day before. He was now checking on me after I spent a day under anaesthesia.

I looked at him and asked about Khaled – for all the blood I had lost, I begged him to tell me something about my blood brother. He remained quiet though, then answered my question, as if the fact that I hadn't seen Khaled for so long weren't enough indication that something grim had happened.

I barely managed to ask, 'What the hell! Where's Khaled? I can't see him! Is he alright?'... From the way he looked at me I could tell he was at pains to answer my question. 'He's okay', he said to calm me down, but this would work only if I could see him, and I could tell that he wasn't doing very well... That twin of my soul, my other half, who healed my first fracture, was hurting me. Restlessly, I lay on the bed wishing I could do something for him, anything, when he was so far away, while my breath came ragged and heavy and pain was consuming me with God knows what wounds.

In the al-Sakhour area hospital, thirst was gnawing at my throat. Since no one answered my first request despite my desperate attempts, I asked again, but even water was not easy to obtain. The doctor said that I had undergone three operations in the stomach and in my legs, and that I was prohibited from drinking water for a designated period... He tried to alleviate my suffering by moistening a piece of cloth and wiping my lips and my face with it.

The paramedics and the doctors formed a circle around my bed, and I grabbed the opportunity to ask them to see Khaled. I was pretty sure he was in some trouble, and I reiterated my request insistently.

'Where is Khaled?' I asked. 'He's good', I was told... But everyone else couldn't help but look at each other as if they were confused by my question... I asked again with greater emphasis, 'Guys, for the love of God, how is Khaled? Why are you standing here? I'm fine, I'm good. Go see Khaled, please'.

I anticipated a number of answers... Khaled is helping the paramedics... Khaled is telling the world about your injury... Khaled is wounded... or perhaps... Khaled... is gone... he left without bidding you adieu... he broke the promise between you two... and died a martyr... he preceded you to the place where many beloved ones have gone too, so many of them that one wishes they would die themselves... But I didn't want to hear any of that... I wanted Khaled's voice... and when I say Khaled's voice I mean his voice, his voice alone... free of the effects of a shrapnel or a wound... telling me that he's good, and I believe him, then I surrender to a deep slumber until my body is healed or I gasp my last... I wanted to see him come in through the door, panting at his concern over my condition, not because of his own wounds. It would have sufficed to hear his laughter, the same that cheered us up in the hardest moments, but somehow this remained within the realm of my imagination.

'Khaled was hit in his head by some shrapnel...'

I sounded like a wounded man's mother as I said to them, 'Bring him here, or take me to him…'

'No way, your condition doesn't allow it'.

It didn't take me too long to understand how severe the situation was, but still, I couldn't bring myself to accept it. My heart is replete with wounds. It was as if history repeated itself. The same wound from my friend being taken away the first time is now weaponised toward the friend who extended his hand and pulled me out of a seemingly endless misery in which that tragedy had plunged me. They said it was just shrapnel in his head, but the outcome was a nightmare which I was going to spend the rest of my life trying to wake up from, hoping to find out it was all a mirage. Oh God, I wish you had done all that to me and me alone to endure, so that Khaled could carry on with the journey.

The paramedics tried to calm me down. They realised how much Khaled meant to Hadi. They loved him as much as they loved Hadi. But how could my heart find consolation and how could my grief heal as long as I could only see him in my imagination? If it hadn't been for my mother begging, hopefully, for updates, how could I find any relief? People around me could hardly hold back the tears.

In those days, the pain and suffering weren't confined to my body on my bed. My family in Türkiye were in a state of restlessness as reports of the explosion flooded social media pages. Everyone wanted a piece of news about Hadi Abdullah. Is he still alive or did the hateful bomb make him a martyr for the sake of keeping the Revolution's flame alight? But Hadi didn't want to talk to anyone, so severe had the blow been, so shattering for my heart as the source of my speech and for my mind as the organ that put my words together before I uttered them. My family had to be content with the news and the pictures they received from the paramedics, but I didn't know whether they were relieved to know that I was still alive or whether they became even more agitated by the severity of the injuries all over my body.

On that hospital bed, I fluctuated between consciousness and uncon-sciousness. I would pass out and then emerge as if being pulled out once again from under the rubble, as if the same accident happened over and over again. One day, as I was waking up and opening my eyes again, someone told me that Ra'ed wanted to talk to me. I grabbed the phone and quickly got to the point: 'Ra'ed I'm fine… Khaled's condition is much worse than mine, you guys need to leave Aleppo as soon as possible'. I then pushed the phone away from me. I could hear the sighing in his voice. He was in Türkiye too, but I couldn't say anything else to him. He also ran out of words in his dictionary, while far away from him the two of us, his 'kids', lay in bed with severe injuries.

Via Dolorosa

Have you ever heard about the love of the thirsty guy who almost died of thirst? Have you heard about the yearning of the sick for healing? About the blind man's longing to see the sky! By God, my love for him was way greater than that all!

From the time I had arrived at the hospital, I had been putting everyone around me in danger. As soon as the regime found out I was there, they started threatening to bomb it. The situation was beyond unendurable. We needed an alternative solution, and we decided to make our way from the bleeding homeland into Türkiye.

I would open my eyes, as though I was waking up from a coma, in order to fill my lungs with the hope that Khaled could be saved. Then I would go back into my abyss of nonexistence. When I opened my eyes once, my maternal uncle from al-Qusayr was standing in front of me, and he said that he was going to help me leave Aleppo. I could only think of my dear friend though. 'Get Khaled out of the city', I said immediately. My uncle reassured me that Musafer, Khaled's uncle, was also in the same hospital and that he would help transfer Khaled too. That somehow comforted me, but the prospect of loss was still haunting me... Ra'ed's tears couldn't make Khaled come out of his coma, nor could they alleviate my suffering.

However, the only available path to get out of Aleppo was the Castello Road, which wasn't safe. Snipers monitored it, and it was bombed regularly. Before we set off, I asked for strong painkillers such as morphine. The plan was to put me on a mini truck that was more appropriate for the unevenness of the road ahead, but since I was unable to bend my knees, I couldn't get in. Instead, they found an ambulance, loaded me onto it, and thus began a gruelling journey along a dirt road parallel to Castello Road – one that aimed to deliver my shattered body to a country where treatment might restore me to a functioning human being once more.

On these dirt roads, which would be an understatement to describe as being uneven, it takes approximately three hours to get to Türkiye. Although I spent those hours half asleep, I could still feel the roughness of that road, as though I was crawling on it. I was lying down, which didn't help alleviate my pain. In fact, when I capsized off the bed a couple of times, I thought I was drawing my last breath. However, my destiny kept the Angel of Death away from my soul as it reminded me that the road to glory is an impressive, arduous and painful one, and cannot be crossed without suffering and sacrifice.

As expected, something did happen. The road was not suitable for an ambulance, which caused a puncture to one of the tires, but since my transfer couldn't be put off any longer, the driver carried on driving.

I thought about Khaled the whole time. His presence and the joy that it brought; his absence, and how difficult it was to bear it. I prayed that he was able to doze off as a relief from the pain. I found solace in the idea that pain is an aspect of human life. If he was in pain, then he was alive. A little time, along with God's grace, would be enough to bring him back to me. I couldn't get him out of my head, I saw him standing in front of me, his spirit squeezed my heart, and I found myself saying his name every time my tongue uttered a sound. His absence was the disease, his presence the unattainable treatment.

After much bustle and commotion, we had to wait at the Syrian-Turkish border for a whole hour during which I was conscious only half of the time. Later, the doctors at the Iskenderun hospital conducted the necessary x-ray tests on my body, changed my bandages and I was then transferred to the university hospital in Antakya.

What can a mother's heart say upon laying eyes on her beloved son torn apart before her arms can get hold of him? What could a sister say upon seeing his body covered with blood, when they had shared so many good times together, while there's no remedy for it but to share this bitterness too? And what can the sigh of another friend, Ra'ed, reveal but yearning, anxiety, or concern, knowing that a portion of his heart rests on another bed, grappling with death? This is what I saw as I went in and out of consciousness. People crying while I wept for Khaled without shedding a tear. I would involuntarily call his name every time my lips parted. Then, as I returned to the present time and place, I would say his full name and then ask about him. But the hardest questions are the ones that cannot be answered. Whatever ends with an open question mark leaves no chance of appeal.

Martyr Without Permission

They had no other choice but to tell me what happened. Khaled had joined Tarad in death without consulting me... And why should a martyr seek permission from the living for his ascent?

I became flooded with feelings of bewilderment and despair. The whole world looked grim to me. I felt my sorrows weren't sorrows. Pain didn't hurt anymore. Hope no longer mattered! Everything stopped in that moment. Time as a concept vanished and disappeared. In that moment, I was murdered once again. My friends, murder isn't to be buried under the ground; after all, how many souls are shattered dozens of times because of the loss of someone who's so dear to them, dearer than their own soul... how many are buried while they're still alive...?

I wasn't alone, but I was overcome with a feeling of loneliness.

Every time I bent my shoulders, Ra'ed picked me up and held me high. Every time I had my chin upon my chest, my brother Munzer would make me look up. Every time I shed a tear, Tareq would turn it into dew. Every time I said, 'what if,' my family was the best support I could count on. Having said that, the recovery was tough, and my injuries were painful as much as they were serious, to the extent that Ra'ed passed out one day upon seeing my leg as they were changing the bandages. The two long months I spent in bed felt like a life sentence. My broken legs were wrapped in splints, something which I felt my shattered heart also needed the most. And when I felt some relief at the idea of using a wheelchair, hoping it would enable me, I realised I missed him so much. I had turned into useless ashes that could do nothing for the Revolution.

I was transferred to a hospital in Ankara, where I was never alone. Shadi, Munzer, Suhayl, Mas'oud, Marishal (Tarad's brother) and others took shifts to stay in my room. Ra'ed was also planted on the chair next to my bed all the time, unwaveringly looking after me; he refused to sleep and get the rest he needed. He fed me, he washed my face every morning, he carried me to the toilet and kept me company while the nurses, painfully for me, changed my bandages. I underwent a total of nine surgeries, some on my legs and some on my stomach. There was always the risk of kidney failure because one of my kidneys had stopped functioning, which affected the performance of the other one. And yet, despite all the pain and the constant presence of friends and family, Khaled's absence was as evident and piercing as the sun.

Meeting the Martyr

At this point, all areas of Aleppo were under siege. The regime took Castello Road too, the same road I took when I was evacuated, the same road that – despite being quite dangerous – had proven so useful to smuggle in food and medicine and to evacuate the wounded. Hundreds of thousands of civilians were under siege in the same city that I was forced to leave. The horrific massacres against civilians took place non-stop, as though they were a symphony that the crooks took pleasure in. The frequency of the bombings was no longer counted by the day, so numerous were the targets that the injuries and losses were being tallied by the minute... While all this was taking place, I was tied to a bed in a hospital. Hospitals and entire residential areas were wiped out with chlorine gas, so that those who weren't bombed or shot, suffocated to death... all the while, the lump in my throat became bigger.

Desperate times call for drastic measures. Somehow, I thought, I had to get out. Even though I was in a wheelchair, and going back to Syria wasn't going to heal my wounds, the battle to free Aleppo from its siege had just started on its outskirts. I was hoping to be able to join the rebels and show them my sympathy for their endurance and their victory. I was also hoping to be able to visit Khaled's grave. I checked with the doctor, and he told me not to take any risks. All my family and friends tried to dissuade me from going; Ra'ed alone understood and endorsed my decision without hesitation.

He drove with me to the border between Türkiye and Syria, then to Kafranbel where Hamoud greeted us with warm tears and long hugs, as though it were our very first day of mourning. On our first night in Kafranbel, a warplane crossed the sky and broke the sound barrier. I woke up in terror. For a second, I forgot that I was injured, and I tried to stand on my feet to run away from a possible bombing. I couldn't, so Ra'ed and Hamoud took me to a less dangerous place where I was able to sleep all night. What a tough and lovely morning it was when I visited the grave of my brother, the one I never thought I'd lose. I spoke to him from my wheelchair for more than two hours. I reprimanded him, told him my secrets, and implored him. His absence felt like a prank too immature to land right. I told him that millions of people knew about him, that even strangers wept for him, anyone with a sense of dignity and affinity to our cause mourned him. I told him most people don't accomplish in their lifetimes a portion of what he had accomplished in his prime. All the while, I felt that as I spoke, he listened and understood me.

August 2016 – the grave of Khaled, the martyr
'I hold your soul in my heart, Khaled, wherever I go. You didn't die. You never will. In twenty years, you achieved more than most people could. You achieved glory, Khaled. You had an aim, and you accomplished it. Your laugh spread happiness and joy among us. And it still will. Your laughter will be our guiding light. The people responsible for your death won't sleep. They killed you because your activism was a thorn in their side, and I promise you that it will still haunt them. We will get rid of them. As long as your soul is with me, we will be together in this endeavour'.

I will keep laughing, despite everything. Leaving the path that we took would amount to a betrayal.

The Journey of Recovery and Homesickness

After visiting Khaled – may God rest his soul – I headed back to Aleppo with Munzer and Ra'ed, to the city's battlefronts where the battle to break the siege was taking place. We tried to get to the front line. Ra'ed and Munzer helped me get out of the car and put me in the wheelchair. We set up and properly carried out an interview with one of the military commanders. Ra'ed was getting old and yet he worked so hard to make sure I had everything I needed, despite him being injured himself, and he held the camera to replace Khaled. He even helped me with the video editing.

The battle saw the rebels prevail, and their victory had the effect of a balm that relieved the severity of our wound. Meanwhile, Ra'ed was stationed at another battlefront to make up for the shortage of people, undeterred by the grim feelings that the recent events had produced. After spending four days in Syria, which certainly helped me with the pain and suffering and allowed me to take my mind off my worries, we went back to Türkiye so I could complete my treatment. As some-one who had always looked down on anyone who professed chauvinist nationalism, I realise that being reinvigorated by my country's air and soil might sound contradictory coming from me. Forced displacement changes everything – enjoying the embrace of your homeland becomes a luxury, exile keeps you away from the ones you love, and spilled blood nurtures the flower of freedom.

In Ankara, I resumed the treatment, which involved having more surgery performed on my legs, followed by a period of recovery which helped the remodelling of my bones. Then I rented a place to stay, and my mood was at an all-time low. I kept reminding myself of the tragedy of losing Khaled, the only glimpse of beauty in that hell that Tarad's departure had made for me. The only solution was for me to be reunited with them. Death was all I could see.

And doesn't death envelop us all? Those who left their childhood home or neighbourhood, whose friends and families are separated from them by borders and seas, and whose dreams are hampered by their circumstances... or those whose souls were separated from their bodies by shrapnel... wasn't death devastating for all these people? Why shouldn't I die too? I can no longer take any more grief. I ought to find a way to silence it all. No noise. No texture. No whining. Just an eternal sleep that leaves no marks on my soul, as the wounds did before. I ruled out the idea of jumping off a building, because my feet couldn't have assisted me in climbing all the way to the top. I thought about poison, or being hit by a car...

The first time I wore those huge post-op shoes and was able to walk with the help of a crutch, I decided that the time had come. I caught Ra'ed and my brother Munzer off guard and sneaked out to the park. I stood on the side of the motorway and decided that this was it, and as I looked and picked the car that I would throw myself in front of, all the images materialised at once in my head.... the corpses, the destruction, the screaming and the black nights... I remembered my promise to Khaled, and the other guys whom I loved too... I remembered that night when we all made a commitment never to give up until the Revolution triumphs in our country or die... I remembered the pledge that we made... I couldn't take my own life.

I went back with even more determination to complete my journey. I felt reborn. Day after day, my dedication to the treatment and the physiotherapy made me walk again. And although my heart was still in pieces, Ra'ed took it upon himself to mend it. This was a hard task for him, but he undertook it with dedication as he was determined to achieve the best outcome in the shortest time possible. He would set out to go filming with me, despite being tired, and he would gather all his strength undeterred by his declining health. He had several bullet wounds, and his respiratory system was compromised following his attempted murder by ISIS in 2013, but he was so resilient he made me forget and move on. He worked with me on the media coverage until I found new partners for my fundamental task: documenting the events until the Revolution bears its fruits.

I started experiencing a new form of fear, and I went back to square one emotionally; I try to pretend that people don't really matter to me, that they're just temporary in my life, but deep down, I'm just afraid of losing them again.

Handless

February 2017

'Incredible Russian madness in Ma'arrat al-Nu'man! We have lost count of the Russian airstrikes. Houses have been burned or razed. Martyrs have been incinerated to death, while some are still buried under the debris. All the while, the airstrikes hit the same targets more than once. By God, this is beyond words'.

'The mixed feelings of fatigue, frustration and disgust will kill us all! We feel helpless and unable to do anything substantial about al-Ghoutah... to alleviate the suffering of its people, to comfort them in any way. The commanders of the Northern armed groups shamelessly hitting each other while al-Ghoutah is being slaughtered.

'And we are being slaughtered too, our hearts bleeding for each drop of blood spilt by its children. Our hearts go out to their mothers with every cry of fear and terror they let out.

'We die with each martyr that falls, then we come back to life and die again of helplessness and sorrow'.

October 2017

Every time I thought I had become desensitised and toughened up, or I felt covering the events and conveying them to the world had become pointless, something happened that revived the humanity I had lost throughout seven years of Revolution.

The day after the massacre at the vegetable market in Ma'arrat al-Nu'man, as I walked among the corpses and smelled the odor of blood everywhere, I saw a severed human hand on a box of green apples.

I contemplated this sight for a long while... was it the seller's hand? Or did it belong to a father who was buying apples for his children (they waited for him to come home, but he didn't)? The sight of the severed hand stirred my humanity, the one I lost at the gates of history.

I cried, and I felt that it was my own hand that had been cut off, betrayed and oppressed. I felt we had all become handless, unable to bring the apples home to those children that had been worn out by the bombing and exhausted by the massacres.

It was the hand of a world incapable of stopping the ongoing carnage in Syria.

The Pledge Renewal

15 March 2018

The seventh anniversary of the Revolution.

To Bashar al-Assad and to all the world's tyrants.

To Putin and Hassan Nasrallah, and to all the militias that fight for them.

We stand before you, we won't be defeated, we won't surrender.

In the eighth year of the never-ending Revolutions, we begin a new life and devote it to our cities in ruins, we make history with our blood and we consign the names of the martyrs to the archives of eternity.

To whom this may concern, today we clench the Revolution as if it were an ember, we name our country after it to make it become timeless, for our land to cling to life.

We resist, undeterred by the wounds on our bodies, despite our souls having ascended to heaven.

We resist, in the conviction we will never forget the massacres and that we will hold onto the pictures of the rightful martyrs who have lined up on the path to heaven.

We resist until the last drop of blood, and we have no doubt in the righteousness of the armed rebellion and its *takbirs*.

On the anniversary of the Revolution, as our night has darkened, our hearts have been shattered, and despite stumbling over our tears, and the misery of our mothers, our women, and our children.

On the anniversary of the Revolution, as helplessness has overcome us, and the loss of loved ones has exhausted us.

We have no other option but to choose it again, and again and again, forever, we shall never give up on it... It's the course, the life, the war we have chosen, it's the values that we live by and die for.

On the anniversary of the Revolution, we shall remain loyal to the first outcry and shall keep shouting until the break of dawn.

Out with you, Bashar!

A Crazy Idea

Every person's path is determined, and they walk hand in hand with their cause. No matter how much grief and longing storm through us, and no matter how much we suffer from loss and separation, sweet memories remain a beacon of strength to endure the hardships of the path.

Take Rahaf. The war that took her life has bequeathed a new sister with her qualities, one that plays with her siblings in a park in Türkiye until it's safe for them to embrace their homeland again.

For every flower that wilts, two blossom. And for every bud withered by the drought, the dew nurtures ten. We went back to our cherished office in the motherland, Syria, and Ra'ed started accompanying me again to cover events. The massacres became our everyday bread, we became accustomed to witnessing a lot of them. This kind of work was not suitable for Ra'ed at all, but he selflessly endured his weakened condition and never moaned about it. At one point he recommended to me two new workmates, Muhammad Daher, who had been in charge of the media centre in Ma'arrat al-Nu'man, and Ali Dandoush, who had already moved in with us after working at Radio Fresh. He couldn't have recommended a better pair of guys, strong and courageous on the frontlines, but also so compassionate and sympathetic with me. In time, that same fear of loss manifested inside me again. I started worrying about my colleagues and about Ra'ed too, and I was at a loss. That same nightmare was keeping me up again. In Ma'arrat al-Nu'man we converted our friend Abu Arab's house into a media operations room in which I had meetings with friends and fellow activists Hussam, Mu'az, Azo and Daher. From there, we would set off to cover the events in the liberated north. In Kafranbel, on the other hand, I was with Ra'ed, Hamoud, Abdallah, Ali and a bunch of lovely people, relatives and old friends of Ra'ed's with whom we would spend peaceful extended evenings, lingering after long hours of work.

Slowly life began smiling at me again. I devoted most of my time to the beloved cause of the Revolution, whose path made tragedy become bearable. On the other hand, we kept getting threats, sometimes by the regime, who implied that it was going to wipe out Idlib, where many members of the opposition lived, and sometimes from ISIS, who were determined to decapitate me and Ra'ed and put up our severed heads on Kafranbel's main roundabout. The most serious threats, however, came from Jabhat al-Nusra, who made it clear to us that they were not going to arrest us this time, but kill us straightaway. They accused us of conducting social work without their authorisation, work that we continued in the face of their destruction, forced displacement and intimidation. With the increase in the number of threats, we had to adapt to the new reality, and we got into the habit of changing our residences regularly to prevent any unexpected raids. In the meantime, Ra'ed had been planning something completely different and raised the possibility of me getting married. I, whose heart was already tormented by the losses, how could I even reasonably contemplate the possibility of bringing someone else into this life of mine?

A Non-Critical Condition

20 June 2018

Getting married was not a priority for me. I hadn't met anyone who would be able to soothe my wounds. I wasn't sure I was in the right state, given that my heart was telling me it was dead and that there is no room for innocent romance in a time of war. Who would be willing to share my heart with the Revolution? Who would be willing to be the life companion of a ghost who put his life on the line with every news report? A shadow, whose daily meal was death, the smell of which he inhaled with every cigarette? But Ra'ed insisted. He said it was overdue. He said it with the authority of a parent, the affection of a sibling and the concern of a friend, and he carried out the quest for the awaited bride himself. Meanwhile, I avoided the subject, cancelled, and postponed... I still kept the doors of my heart shut... a fortress. Every time he came to talk to me about marriage, I would shake my head in refusal or simply dodge his questions... Ra'ed was someone to be trusted, a virtuous son of the Revolution that only gives birth to heroes... it didn't take him too long to bring me the news. 'You have nothing to lose, and you don't have to accept but at least agree to see her'. He said this to me with utter sincerity, as though she were the gardenia of life that was destined to sprout right in the heart and be the bloom to brighten my life... And yet, I didn't want to see her. What was the point if I didn't want to get married in the first place? I'm not good at pretending, and

I didn't want to waste anyone's time. Except Ra'ed wouldn't budge, and he eventually took me to see her against my will.

The first time we met, I found her to be as lovely as I had been told her to be, a sweet and great conversationalist. No sooner had I seen her than my fortress of a heart turned into an orchard. After a few minutes, she was all I could see. When we looked at each other, the feeling was beyond words. Ra'ed couldn't believe it when I told him that I agreed in principle. Love is like a tempest. There were no clouds in my sky to bring this rain, but since when does rain need the sky's permission to fall anyway?

We started talking and meeting regularly and sharing confidences like two mirrors facing one another, and as we got to find out more about each other, our hearts were open books. Our eyes sparked every time we talked, the feeling of hands almost touching when you run closely alongside someone. Next, we decided to get engaged and let everyone know that we wanted to get married. We rushed the preparations for the reading of Surah al-Fatiha so much and with such enthusiasm that none of my family and relatives managed to attend... No one expected things to take this turn, so Ra'ed and Hamoud tirelessly took care of all major and minor details. We bought the rings and Ra'ed's cousins, headed by Fateh Shaykh, acted as my own family for the purpose of the engagement, which took place at the bride's house. I couldn't have hoped for a more wonderful group of people.

We saw each other more and more frequently, until the hours of daytime were no longer enough for us, and we couldn't bear staying away from each other. Silence became particularly intolerable. We missed each other's voices especially during the night, until finally meeting up made the waiting worthwhile. All we needed to be pronounced man and wife was to finalise the religious part of the marriage. My mother and my siblings entered Syria to come to the wedding from Türkiye, and so did most of my extended family. Those who couldn't be there sent someone on their behalf to bring their love, as a flower sends its scent, like Khaled's mother – my other 'mother' – who honored us with her presence (and her *zaghroutas*), and Tarad's brother, Muwaffaq, who also joyfully joined us. All this in the spirit of the Revolution and its unique ability to inspire and amplify love, to celebrate the groom and his 'Rafah' and wish them to be blessed with children. Ra'ed and Hamoud deserved most of the credit for the success of the event; they tirelessly went around looking after everything, from hospitality to the religious procedures officiated by the sheikh, and much more. Before I knew it, I was holding hands in front of everybody with the man who was now my father-in-law; meanwhile, the *zaghroutas* rose in the air undeterred by the war and its efforts to smother them.

What a wonderful moment for the father. The apple of his eye, the joy of his heart, and the light of his home, his little baby was now getting married. He found someone to entrust her to and to honour their bond and preserve their mutual affection, as if saying to me, take her, take my heart, but don't you ever dare to make her eyes shed a single tear. I felt my heart would come out of my chest, honoured as I was to carry that responsibility. I was no longer alone in my life. Rafah became my refuge, and I, her strength. Love prevailed.

When the Revolution broke out, my father-in-law had not remained neutral, which I suppose made our handshake even firmer. Whereas a great deal of my fellow revolutionaries had their marriage proposals turned down because of their activism and lack of stability, my wedding was empowering in this sense, a new seed sown in a fertile land from which freedom will spring, no matter the cost. In the early days of the Revolution, my father-in-law shot several videos, his house was burned following an airstrike and he survived by some miracle. Rafah herself joined the women's protests and demonstrated against the tyrannical regime.

We didn't think it was appropriate to have *dabkeh* dancing at our wedding, considering the massacres that were being perpetuated against civilians.

After the wedding, I rented a little place near the radio station and got it ready for our little family to move in. Once the religious ceremony had taken place, I visited more and more frequently, and we went out to have a good time together. Unfortunately, my family couldn't obtain an entry permit into Syria, and they did not make it to the traditional *zaffeh* reception, which took place sometime after the ceremony and was officiated by Ra'ed, Tarad's brother and Khaled's mother. Much as everyone went out of their way to have the best celebration possible, I couldn't help thinking of those who weren't with us.

Two Arrows in the Heart

October 2018

Two days after my wedding, I was ready to go back to work at the media office despite the sleeplessness which that entailed, but Ra'ed instead proposed that I go to visit my family in Türkiye to spend a few days with them. My wife and I departed at once and after a long time, we were reunited with my family. Words cannot describe how excited they were. They were so relieved after all the worries to see me in the company of my wife. At the same time, I couldn't be idle and soon resumed working on a social services project that we had set up in Türkiye, keeping in touch and liaising with Ra'ed, Hamoud and the rest. 'We miss you, *ishta'nalak*', they kept saying, 'when are you coming back?' Much as I was delighted to see my family, I felt like a fish out of water and couldn't wait to go back to my habitat.

One day, I left my phone at home and went out to run a few errands. When I came home that Friday at noon (23 November 2018), I found dozens of missed calls on my phone. I was always sort of ready to receive bad news, but this was different. My heartbeats surged with intensity, and I sighed deeply preparing for the worst. Long story short, I was informed that Ra'ed and Hamoud had suffered an attempt on their lives and had been rushed to the hospital. Hamoud was dead, and Ra'ed's situation was critical. Soon I started getting the pictures and I could hardly breathe. I wasn't ready for that; I could barely stand on my feet. A white Kia Rio had been tailing Ra'ed lately, until on Friday, a van cut off the car in which Ra'ed, Hamoud and Ali Dandush were riding...

At that point a group of men jumped from the vehicle and unloaded on them, most of their shots landing on Ra'ed and Hamoud.

Final report: Ra'ed and Hamoud are now both martyrs.

The details: no further details, no words can grasp the grief, the human mind cannot comprehend what is happening.

Ra'ed and Hamoud's departure took away the last ounce of hope from my existence.

My brothers were killed for no reason other than being sons of the Revolution. Murdered by a bunch of cowards who couldn't even show their faces.

The destiny of our Revolution's heroes is to be killed by some bastards!

They joined Khaled, Tarad and the other martyrs...

I wonder what they looked like when they met. How did Khaled greet them? Which other martyrs did he introduce them to? Are they at ease now? What are they thinking? Did they talk about me at all? About Kafranbel? About the wretches who killed them? Did Khaled introduce them to Tarad? Did Khaled and Tarad talk about me?

Inadvertently, I thought about calling Ra'ed to ask him what to do. Who is going to be my mentor and my guide now? Who am I going to turn to for help?

I made quick plans to attend their funeral and kiss their foreheads for the last time, but travelling proved more difficult than I thought, and I didn't make it. I missed Tarad's funeral in Lebanon and couldn't go to Khaled's in Kafranbel because my legs were shattered. Now these two had left me without saying goodbye. That ray of hope that I mentioned at the beginning of this book faded out before I reached its conclusion. Alas, I had not seen the light at the end of the tunnel, and life became increasingly more difficult to navigate. As if Tarad had entrusted me to Khaled, and Khaled to Ra'ed... and in turn, Ra'ed didn't want to leave before he had himself found me my soulmate Rafah to walk the tunnel with me until the last day.

I Shall Return

When I went to Syria, Abdallah picked me up at the border crossing. That same border that knew our group so well now longed for our presence. I hugged him as if I was hugging him, Ra'ed and Hamoud all in one. We wept and our cries rose in unison, but soon enough we resumed our duty: crying wasn't going to bring them back. The best thing to do was to look after the social service projects that Ra'ed had been administering, in order to preserve his sweet memory. For every idea he had, he could mobilise an army of guys committed to the cause of the Revolution and the homeland. It was a hard task, but eventually everything fell into place, and I went back to that same room where I could still feel the presence of Ra'ed, Khaled and Hamoud... it was as though we all went back there together. As soon as I returned, the threats resumed. I tried to limit my movements as much as I could, but one day, my wife and I had to go to the doctor for her to receive a medically induced abortion of twin foetuses, due to the difficult personal circumstances we were going through. As we were on our way there, a white Kia Rio was tailing us, the same kind of car that shadowed Ra'ed and Hamoud. It was tough but I managed to lose them. I also realised that I was their next target. Later that day, the same white car and a van came back to our neighborhood. I let my closest friends know about this and asked them to protect us. Our lives were on the line, and everyone suggested that my wife make her way to Türkiye. Somehow every time

I returned, I got sent back... another, even sourer evacuation. I was deprived of the twins, of Kafranbel and of the scent of my homeland: the thought of these three things together brought me to tears as I crossed the border. My heart was weary, my mind restless and busy thinking... I was flooded with sadness and slipping into depression. I was torn between the fear for my wife's life, the apprehension about the work that I left behind and my friends, who were dying one after the other... I couldn't stay with my hands tied... that's how I am, even if I lost my legs I would crawl back. Death is the easiest thing to face in a situation like this... that's why I decided to return. I told myself, even if they send me back a thousand times, I will still return until my promise is fulfilled, or the covenant expires.

The Phobia of Loss

In Türkiye, the days passed at a very slow pace. I was surrounded by my family, which gave me a sense of peacefulness and prosperity, yet something was sticking in my throat. I felt like I was choking. My promise to Tarad, my pledge with Khaled, and my loyalty to Ra'ed and Hamoud, were like a rope pulling me towards Syria.

Tarad, Khaled, Hamoud, Ra'ed and the Revolution! The thought of these five wore me out and rendered me fragile. I deliberately mention the people first and then the Revolution, because they represented the only thing left that was worth sacrificing for.

Before them, I had been in the prime of life, building my dream brick by brick... and every time I laid the last brick, an airstrike hit it and brought it down. As we climbed into bed every night, I hoped that the next day would bring news of relief... and that one day, it didn't matter how distant in the future, we would thankfully look back and praise God, because faith in Him is never in vain.

They were gone before we finished our work. We were supposed to walk together the path of our Revolution, the one to which we committed our lives. We were like a single flag, yet blown in disparate directions by the wind. It was not meant to be.

And nevertheless, the wall shall be built, and a tall building shall be erected, for its bricks will be molded with blood and selflessness. Virtuous hands and noble spirits will tirelessly and resiliently build it.

A New Chapter

I talked to myself again, and the internal dialogue wouldn't end: No matter how bad the situation is, the worst thing they can do is kill me! Here I am, dying in exile a thousand times over, anyway. I spiral within my own thoughts, almost going delirious. I've got more friends in paradise than ever before. What do I have to fear now?

I crossed the border into Syria, this time determined never to leave again until I die. May God spare me the pain of separation and the bitterness of exile!

I went back to my old digs, next to the radio station. Before we knew it, airplanes of different nationalities appeared, as though one wasn't enough to torment us; fifteen jets would hover above us at the same time, bomb all their targets and systematically scorch the entire area. Normally, I would go out to cover the resulting massacres. This one time though, I was supposed to set off to work on a reportage on the wider military developments and to conduct an interview with Jaysh al-'Izza's commander Jamil al-Saleh. The whole thing happened very quickly, but before I headed over there, I told Rafah that she and her family had to evacuate the house right away and leave Kafranbel. Somehow, I had the feeling that the situation was getting worse and going out of control, especially after several raids were carried out over the previous days in our neighbourhood.

Rafah was pregnant for the second time and, after what happened to

Tarad, Khaled, Ra'ed and Hamoud, I became even more fearful and apprehensive about her as well as about my two new workmates, Abdallah the Crocodile and Muhammad Daher. At half past four, approximately forty-five minutes after the house was evacuated, a cluster rocket struck it.

When I came home from Hama, I found the whole place razed, its doors scattered around. It looked as if an uninvited guest had visited and spread his depravity across all corners.

Given how anxious I had become, I was relieved only when I noticed that some of our personal effects were missing, which led me to think that Rafah packed and took them with her. She settled with her family in an area near the border with Türkiye, where over a million Syrians were living to save themselves from the airstrikes. I promised her that I would be more careful and not put my life in danger. I wanted to live long enough to see the birth of our daughter.

Up until this attack, we had been staying in Kafranbel. Then we moved to Haas first and then to Ma'arrat al-Nu'man. People kept getting disheartening news of massacres, so I set out to prepare a military report highlighting the steadfastness of the rebels fighting against Assad's army. This coincided with the liberation of Hammamiyyat, a village in the Hama province, which had never been taken by the rebels before but was an important stronghold of the Assad regime due to its strategic upland location.

That same evening, I agreed with Muhammad Daher, Jamil and two other guys from near Aleppo, Ammar and Rami, that we would leave at dawn the next day because airstrikes were less likely to take place until approximately 8 a.m. The next morning, we set out, passing through several dangerous points in Khan Shaykhoun, Morek, Kafr Zita, arriving at Hammamiyyat at five-thirty in the morning. We found traces of a fierce battle, with damaged tanks and craters from rockets and raids everywhere. We needed, first and foremost, to avoid the dirt roads, which were filled with landmines. We took our precautions and carefully chose the appropriate framing to capture the hill and the sides of the battle, but before we could even leave the car, an airstrike hit five or six metres away from us. We got out of the car and ran in different directions. That was only the start. Another strike followed soon after, with planes flying so frighteningly low that we thought they were going to land on our heads. In addition, we were being targeted by heavy artillery and five or six rocket launchers, which managed to set the area on fire and surround it with clouds of dust. I came to my senses lying flat with my chest to the ground, heedless to the stones scarring my legs. Naturally, being under such intense shelling, scattered around as we were, we were unable to document any of what was happening. Filming was no longer possible, and we had to prioritise our own safety.

As I lay on the ground, my breath mixed with the smoke and dust. My heart pounded with terror for my two companions, and for my partner in life, separated from me by battles and warzones, while peace dwelled in her eyes, and hope grew quietly within her. We couldn't crawl to get out of there or to at least reach one another. We couldn't get to the car. I shouted to no avail and realised that even communicating with each other had become nearly impossible. In the middle of all this madness, I saw visions of our unborn daughter behind a small trench, and I called out to God earnestly to let me live and see her with my own eyes.

In the meantime, we heard cries for help and moved in their direction until we realised they came from the rebel fighters. We crawled, and ran, and rolled on the ground until somehow, we reached them. They were four, their faces covered in blood, one of them suffering from a serious injury to his leg. They stepped on a landmine as they were running from the explosions. We asked them about the ambulances, but they said that there were none and asked us to drive them out. We couldn't all fit in our car, and driving wasn't exactly safe anyway, but some of them needed urgent treatment for their wounds.

We decided to put the wounded in the car, and the rest of us would figure something out until we got to a less dangerous area. We were going to drive them out first and then wait for my media team to catch up with us, but another airstrike took place, and we had no other choice but to head towards Kafar Zita, leaving Muhammad, Jamil, Ammar, and Rami behind. I was torn between the concern for the friends I came with and the wounded that we came upon. We arrived at an orchard between the two areas, flames devouring everything, clouds of smoke rising into the sky. I cried and couldn't stop praying for my friends. My heart couldn't have endured any more loss or grief.

As we were getting ready to go back to rescue Muhammad, Jamil, Ammar, and Rami, some other rebel fighters that we encountered in the orchard strongly advised against it, because they knew that our car was being tracked using the Kornet target tracker missiles and that the driver and I would never make it out alive if we went back into that area. We were there a few minutes before that, and we thought it was strange how nothing happened to us, which the fighters themselves couldn't explain. They said it was miracle. We didn't know whether we should be happy to be alive or worried about having a target on our backs. Ultimately, we decided to drive for about one kilometre outside of Hammamiyyat and then continue on foot looking for our friends. And that's what we did. We parked the car under a tree in an orchard, and I started screaming into the walkie talkie calling for Muhammad Daher, but he didn't respond. The more his response was delayed, the more fright settled in my heart. The area was full of shelling and shooting, like anger descending upon us from the sky as we moved closer.

After a long wait, we kept getting closer and closer to them until we heard their voices at last, 'We are good'. 'For now'. I told them how we could not bring the car, and that that was why we had to walk to them. When we finally got to where they were, I couldn't believe my eyes when I saw them all there despite the burning danger, knackered like we were. Next thing, we had to bring them out safely from this den of bombs. And as we were making it out of that hell and reached the town of Morek, my phone happened to pick up the signal from the Turkish telephone network and rang. Rafah was calling me at seven in the morning, which was unusual. Something in her heart told her about what had happened and woke her up to check on me. It looks like I won't be able to hide my moves from her in the foreseeable future. God willing, I thought, the future will bring us better prospects, thoughts and challenges.

Inside me, something told me that our story had just begun to unfold.

Part Three 2019-2025

Prologue

The long night of grief never seems to end, and daytime seems only to bring more sorrows. How are we supposed to live our lives as we go from one critical situation to another?

Yet, we committed to stay on our path forever.

Every gloomy heartbeat is followed by a hopeful one. And every heartbeat I skip, the next one makes even more noise as long as I am alive... Someone appeared and became the queen of my heart. She turned the noise of my heartbeats into music, and its stillness into devotion. My lovely Rafah, as lovely as our Revolution, breathed the spirit of the jasmine.

There were more of these critical conditions that we endured for our ongoing Revolution, but they were merely the sound of sighs from the wounds.

As my memory is weary, I have let the words come out naturally. If I am not always eloquent in the way I tell you what happened, that's because I wanted this to be a genuine reflection of what emerged from under the rubble.

Our Darkest Hour

June 2019

We safely got back to our media centre in Ma'arrat al-Nu'man, and found out the other guys were okay. My wife was pregnant with Bissan. I had been incommunicado and could only get in touch with her when I arrived. I thought it was unusual for her to send me so many messages so early in the morning, because I assumed she had been asleep. She had been awake and wanted me to reassure her.

We got the editing of the footage done and uploaded it. The images were horrendous. It was one of the hardest reports to carry out, the first of many like this. Every day ten, twelve Russian warplanes would take off from the Hmeimim airbase near Latakia and bomb multiple areas in the Hama province and the southern part of the Idlib province in the northwest of Syria. A horrible massacre happened in the vegetable market of Ma'arrat al-Nu'man in which dozens of civilians fell and dozens more were injured. Such massacres became the backdrop to our daily lives, which became an endless sequence of bombings, of warplanes, of helicopters dumping barrel bombs on us. All this time I could never see my wife, because she had moved to a safer area near the border with Türkiye.

This was an incredibly dark and demoralising period. We were surrounded by enemies on all sides: the regime and its army, the Russian air force, Hezbollah, Iranian forces, and Iraqi militias. Every day, dozens of our people, both civilians and rebel fighters, were killed as they desperately tried to stop the regime from reclaiming territory that had long been under rebel control. This devastation was largely the result of the stark imbalance between our military and logistical capabilities and those of the regime and its powerful allies. We kept losing territory after territory.

It was during this bleak time that we received news of Abd al-Baset al-Sarout's death. He was one of my closest friends. I met him multiple times in Homs's old quarters, al-Khalediyyeh and al-Bayyadah, where he lived.

Abd al-Baset. How could one possibly sum him up? Even an entire book wouldn't do justice to this iconic figure, a true symbol of the Syrian Revolution. Talal Derki's outstanding documentary *Return to Homs* offers only a glimpse into his remarkable journey. But he meant far more to us than any film could ever capture.

At one point, when both my hometown, al-Qusayr, and Homs were under siege and meeting in person became impossible, I kept in regular contact with him. He inspired me to be strong, courageous, and resilient. He gave it all for the cause of the Syrian revolution, almost recklessly so.

There is a video of him after a serious injury.[10] He was in such pain that they had to sedate him, but he still found the strength to speak – no, to shout – as tears rolled down his cheeks, insisting he still wished to open a safe passage for civilians. Watching this video made an incredible impact on me: there he was, on a hospital bed, suffering excruciating pain, and still thinking of the misery of his fellow citizens.

Like many of us, he suffered under siege and survived eating boiled tree leaves. Later, he was expelled and displaced to northern Homs province, where he endured even more hardship. Eventually, like so many of us, he moved north to Idlib, and I had the chance to meet him more frequently, this courageous, smart, and down-to-earth man whom I watched dig trenches with his bare hands.

❖ ❖ ❖

By June 2019, I was regularly in contact with him. When he moved to a place near Hama, he brought with him not only his personality but also his scars, and his experience living under siege in Homs. Through his actions as much as through his words, he became a tremendous source of motivation and inspiration for all of us, encouraging the people of Syria to resist the Assad regime.

He would even go into clashes barefoot, proving his selflessness, generosity, and manliness. He truly was one in a million. Whenever he visited us in Ma'rrat al-Nu'man or Kafranbel, his very presence was enough to lift the mood and make us forget the misery around us. Amidst everything, he still had the ability to make us laugh, to tell stories, to crack jokes.

The more frequently I met with him, the more I admired him, and the closer we became. There are so many anecdotes worth telling: at 2 or 3 a.m., after unforgettable nights of laughter and genuine friendship, we would invite him to stay over, but no, he would jump on his motorcycle and ride back, in the middle of the night, from Ma'rrat al-Nu'man to Ltamneh in the Hama province.

Before the Revolution, Abd al-Baset was already well-known across Syria as the goalkeeper for the national youth football team. Back then, Ibrahim Alma was the third-choice goalkeeper behind him. (Alma would later become the starter for the Syrian national team, the team we called *the National Barrel Bomb Team*.)

Abd al-Baset also played for al-Karameh, Homs's main football club, which we all rooted for. But when the protests started, he left football entirely to focus on activism. From the earliest days, he stood out as a protest leader, chanting slogans and inventing some of the most creative and inspiring chants not just in Syria, but across the Arab World during the Arab Spring.

❖ ❖ ❖

While many of us, myself included, used pseudonyms and tried to hide our faces, Abd al-Baset always showed his, becoming a target for the regime and a beloved symbol for the people of Homs.

His sacrifice, selflessness, creativity, and spirit really captured everything our Revolution stood for.

Like so many other Syrians, he eventually picked up a weapon, not to seek violence, but to defend his neighbourhood from the regime's shabbihah and to protect the protests. He helped establish the Martyrs of al-Bayyadah Battalion, named after his home neighbourhood in Homs. The days of football and peaceful protests were gone. Although wounded several times, he always found the strength to rise again.

During the siege of Homs, Abd al-Baset suffered unimaginable personal loss: four of his brothers and five maternal uncles were killed. His mother, who lost five sons and five brothers, came to be known as the 'Khansaa' of Syria', a reference to the 7th-century Arab poetess famed for her elegies mourning sons and brothers lost in battle.

One night, we exchanged voice notes, joking to lighten the heaviness of war. I remember we agreed to meet up the next day. That same night, he was gravely wounded and rushed to Türkiye for treatment. But he didn't survive.

Since both our families had settled in the same area in Türkiye, our mothers had also grown close. I had a personal bond with his family, and so I immediately travelled there to retrieve his body and bring him back across the border for burial in Syria.

Burying Abd al-Baset triggered an emotional collapse in me. His death came on the heels of relentless massacres, defeats, and tragedies, dealing a devastating blow to our morale. I fell into a deep depression. The regime's public celebration of his assassination, branding it a victory, only deepened my despair. Covering mass killings while my friends were dying all around me was excruciating.

Our daily routine was gruelling. At 6 a.m., planes and helicopters woke us. We would head out to document the destruction and return home utterly exhausted. Sometimes, a barrel bomb or airstrike would land near our house in the dead of night, jolting us awake. Day after day, we were immersed in death and heartbreak.

Massacres took place across southern Idlib: Jabal al-Zawiyeh, Ma'rrat al-Nu'man, Kafranbel, Hass, Khan Shaykhoun, Khan al-Sabel. From a personal standpoint, perhaps even a selfish one, the bombing of the Radio Fresh building in Kafranbel hit particularly hard. In a video I recorded afterward, I said it felt like Khaled, Ra'ed, and Hamoud had died a second time. The airstrike didn't just kill them, it destroyed their legacy.

Those months were among the hardest we lived through. The regime fully reclaimed the Hama province, followed by the southern parts of Idlib. Day in, day out the regime retook Syria, city after city. This triggered a massive wave of displacement. Hundreds of thousands fled toward the Turkish border, seeking safety. But they were still targeted. The overwhelming influx also strained the area's infrastructure, leaving many unable to reach shelter.

The regime also captured cities that held deep personal significance for me. Kafranbel, where I lived after 2014, fell. Then Ma'rrat al-Nu'man, home to our media centre. That city is unique, not just in Syria, but perhaps in the world. Its long, defiant history earned it a reputation as a phoenix rising from the ashes. Legend says it was burned to the ground seven times and rebuilt each time by its citizens. When it fell, I remember wondering: Will this incredible city, now being burned for the eighth time, this time by Assad and his allies, rise again?

Amid all this, God sent me a light in the darkness: my daughter, Bissan. She was born around that time. What an overwhelming mix of emotions. I had always wanted a daughter. She was born in exile, far from Homs and Kafranbel, her parents' birthplaces.

Shortly after, a fragile ceasefire was imposed by Türkiye, Iran and Russia, which the regime violated whenever it saw fit. We were confined in a small, densely populated area, in the northwest of Syria. We began picking up the pieces. I found a small place for my little family near the Turkish border and tried to build some semblance of normal life, however fragile.

Picking up the Pieces and Starting Again

I want to emphasise this: even in our darkest hour, God the Almighty never abandons us. He always sends something, or someone, that compels us to survive, to keep going, not to give up.

Loss is devastating. Whether it's your family, your closest friends, or even your own home, the one you were forced to flee multiple times, the pain is unbearable. When you've lost everything, when every reason to get out of bed in the morning has vanished, something unexpected still finds its way to you. A ray of light. A source of hope. For me, that was my daughter, Bissan. Bisso, as I call her. She gave me a reason to live.

During the ceasefire, we tried to adjust to our new reality as well as to the psychologically traumatic state we were in. I hope I can convey to Western readers what forced displacement truly means, i.e. when you are torn away from your home, your memories, your dreams, your childhood, everything. I was displaced, uprooted, and I tried to build new dreams, new memories.

Despite everything, we showed remarkable resilience. We threw ourselves into a variety of projects aimed at comforting and supporting the people around us, who were drowning in tragedy and despair. From that small corner of the Idlib province, in Syria's northwest, where we had been confined, we worked to build a 'Little Syria', while the rebels that were with us in the same area prepared to retake the cities the regime had captured.

By then, we were facing many enemies. The Assad regime was only one among several forces that had come to our country to fight us. We often stopped to ask ourselves: *What are these people even doing here?* The Iranians under Qasem Soleimani, the Lebanese Hezbollah, more than seventy Iraqi militias, and the Russian air force. Why were they here? Why were they killing us?

I know those questions are futile, but I couldn't help asking them out of sheer frustration. It felt as though the world's worst criminals had decided to crush us, expel us from our homes, and obliterate our dreams. And yet, what could we do? We had to persevere.

We tried our best to instil hope. But I sometimes questioned my own efforts and activism. Was I selling people false hope? An impossible dream? Realistically, we stood no chance against our enemies. We kept asking our own people to be patient, but we couldn't deliver on our promises.

Still, I told myself that we were standing for justice, that we were on the right side of history, the side of the oppressed against the oppressors. And if dying was the price, then so be it. At least we would die for a just cause. That's why we persisted in trying to light a spark of hope in people's hearts, even as we struggled with our own despair.

We were surrounded by displaced families, hundreds of thousands living in tents along the Turkish border. We had no choice but to be hopeful. Neither we, nor the families arriving in the northwest, had anywhere else to go.

Our work was made even more difficult by the regime's attempts to win back hearts and minds. They had the upper hand: they had retaken most of Syria and crushed our Revolution, branding us as 'terrorists', and had confined us to a small territory. They began sending messages to people inside, trying to lure them back to regime-controlled areas under the guise of 'national reconciliation'.

We had to counter that propaganda. We knew those promises were lies. Accepting them was tantamount to signing our death warrants. I filmed dozens of videos pushing back against that narrative, urging people to uphold their dignity. *Better to die on your feet than live on your knees.* It was a thankless task, perhaps the hardest we faced during that chapter, between 2020 and 8 December 2024. Our mission was to instil not just hope, but also resilience and courage, while staying true to ourselves.

Meanwhile, the armed resistance wasn't idle. Fighters trained, prepared, and focused on self-reliance. They manufactured weapons, drones, they worked hard to become entirely self-reliant. They knew no foreign nation was going to help. When I asked them what message I should pass on to the people, they said: *This time, we're preparing not just to defend ourselves, but to face the regime once and for all. Either we all die, or we are triumphant.*

In parallel, we were building a kind of statelet in the northwest. As revolutionaries and opposition members, we wanted to show the world that we could build something, not just resist. Idlib and its surrounding areas became 'Little Syria' because people from every part of the country had gathered there, from Damascus to Deir Ezzor, from Aleppo to the coast.

We made real progress. People felt safe. The number of killings and robberies plummeted. I, for the first time in years, could walk or drive at night without fear of being arrested or mugged. Public life returned to a semblance of normalcy: markets opened; infrastructure improved. With help from private Turkish companies, we ensured 24-hour electricity, better water quality, and faster internet, luxuries in the rest of Syria even today.

And this made our success even more remarkable, because Idlib had always been an economically neglected region that had no industry, no tourism, and no oil or gas. Yet we managed to build something meaningful. Meanwhile, in regime-controlled areas, people were lucky if they got two hours of electricity a day and their quality of life was much worse. Kidnappings were rampant, and families had to pay massive ransoms to retrieve loved ones. Shabbihah and other regime-linked militias were behind most of these crimes, and they operated with impunity, people such as Suja' al-'Ali who made a name for themselves in this hideous business.

Bissan was growing, and I was becoming increasingly attached to her, perhaps too attached. As you've read in these memoirs, I had developed a deep fear of loss. Everyone I had ever loved was gone. I adored Bissan and became obsessed with her safety. A friend of mine suggested I try to share my love, in other words, to have another child. Bissan was three, and soon after, my wife became pregnant again.

Around that time, I also grew closer to my new circle of friends: Muhammad Daher, Malaz Abu Arab, Jamil Hassan, Muhammad Bel'as, Muhammad al-Faysal, Sa'd Zaydan. We spent a lot of time together, and inevitably, I began to fear losing them too.

As my wife's due date approached, I spent sleepless nights wrestling with a single question: What kind of world am I bringing these children into? Am I doing the right thing?

Then came several offers from the UNHCR office in Ankara. They offered to relocate my family and me to Germany. Then to France. Then Canada. Full legal status, plane tickets, everything. And each time, I said no. I had made a promise to my friends, may God have mercy on their souls, and I was determined to keep it.

But I also asked myself: *am I doing right by my children?* They deserved peace, a normal childhood. Why should they suffer because of my pledge? Why should they be entangled in our Revolution? What did it have to do with them?

I was torn, but I wasn't afraid for myself, only for my children. Yet I couldn't bring myself to leave, I had to carry on. I imagined what Khaled, Tarad, Ra'ed, and Hamoud would think. They wouldn't have approved. I was exhausted, worn down by uncertainty. Though the frequency of attacks had decreased, the threat remained. My wife was nearing her delivery date. Then, the earthquake struck.

Earthquake, the Last Thing We Needed

What I experienced in those few minutes in February 2023 was worse than anything that had come before. It was the last thing we needed.

I had fallen asleep around 3:30 a.m., lying next to my wife. Bissan was asleep in her blue cradle. About an hour later, I felt the bed shaking. At first, I thought it might be shelling, but something was different. It wasn't an airstrike. The building was swaying violently. Windows ripped from their frames. Walls collapsed, one just beside Bissan's cradle.

It was like a scene from a disaster film – but it was horrifyingly real.

We were all half-asleep, I grabbed Bissan and shouted for my wife to move. But she wouldn't, she froze as she didn't understand what was going on. Same as her brother Ahmed, who had been staying with us. Somehow I convinced them to rush outside as the building was about to collapse on top of us.

I realised I had left my phone and car keys upstairs. The tremors had subsided slightly, so I dashed back inside. The flat was in ruins. I grabbed what I could and ran.

Back in the car, I turned to check on Bissan. She was quiet, eyes closed. My heart stopped. Had something struck her? I shook her gently. 'Baby, are you okay?' She started crying. I exhaled. She was alive.

We had nowhere to go. Families stood in the street, many weeping. My wife broke down. One of my friends who lived in a nearby camp rang me. He invited us to stay with him and I accepted. Concrete buildings were more dangerous than tents, so I left my wife and daughter with him and went out to document the aftermath.

It was devastation on a scale I'd never seen. Thousands buried under rubble. Entire neighbourhoods flattened. Chaos everywhere. As if twelve years of war hadn't been enough, we now faced a new horror: death by earthquake. I became even more pessimistic. *Let us all die together and be done with it,* I thought.

The earthquake pushed us back to square one as reporters. We found ourselves covering a disaster of such massive proportions that the country had never witnessed anything like it. Thousands of lives were lost. Hundreds of homes were destroyed. Syria was already on its knees – under siege, under shelling, with no infrastructure or emergency response teams capable of handling a catastrophe of this scale.

And yet, something miraculous happened. The White Helmets coordinated with the local population in such an effective and resourceful way that even modern, prosperous countries would have struggled to match it. Some of our rescue teams managed more cases than those operating in southern Türkiye, despite Türkiye being a fully functioning state. Even the Bab al-Hawa border crossing, the only route through which we could receive vital supplies, was shut down. Staff stationed at the crossing were killed or had lost their homes in the quake. Without bulldozers, ambulances, or medical aid reaching us, we resorted to digging out victims with our bare hands. We had no one else to rely on.

As in the massacres committed by the Assad regime, it felt like it was our fate to be alone.

During the aftershocks, people had no choice but to sleep on the streets. Their homes had become dangerous, unliveable. Tents became easy targets. The regime took advantage of the chaos and struck civilians during these vulnerable moments. We did what we could. We helped the injured. We dug through rubble. We reported. Alongside a team of journalists, I worked relentlessly to raise awareness and gather donations. Meanwhile, since my wife and daughter stayed in a tent with a friend, I hardly saw them at all. I was torn between my duty and my family.

We survived, but at a devastating cost. So many lives lost. So many injured. Amputations, trauma. An earthquake is already difficult in a stable country, let alone in Syria in 2023. What we endured during those February weeks was harder than anything we had lived through in twelve years of revolution. We emerged from it, but we were broken. We picked up the pieces and began again. I set up a tent next to our house while contractors worked on repairs. We couldn't stay inside due to aftershocks. Winter made life in the tent miserable. Strong winds would rip tents apart, and still – we had nowhere to go.

I remember Bissan asking me, 'Why was our house destroyed?'

'Because of the earthquake'.

'But why us?'

I had no answer.

Adnan

Eventually, we repaired the house and resumed life, *life*, in name only. It resembled death in every way. We returned to a kind of routine, but the psychological scars were deep. I would wake in the middle of the night, startled, unsure if I had just felt another tremor. Yet, I also remembered that when Bissan was born, that too had been during a time of hardship. We were being evacuated, confined to Syria's northwest. Her birth had been a ray of hope during overwhelming darkness. After the earthquake, God sent us another ray of hope: my second child, Adnan. I named him after my father. According to Syrian custom, I was already known as *Abu Adnan*, the father of Adnan, even before his birth, since a man traditionally carries his father's name until he has a son of his own.

Adnan brought us the hope we desperately needed. With every new child, I found a new reason to live. Life, however, came with heavier responsibilities. Bissan started nursery, and I began teaching her to read and write. But I also tried to teach her – within the limits of what a three-year-old can grasp – about her origins. About Homs. About our home, with its garden and flowers and birds. I told her one day we would go back.

'Why can't we go now?' she asked.

'Because some bad people, Bashar and his militias, don't let us return to what is rightfully ours', I explained. 'But I promise you, one day we will'.

I wanted her to understand her rights, to know our cause was just. I wanted her to love Homs, even if she had never seen it. I shared this publicly, encouraging others to speak to their children as well. If we couldn't return, maybe our children could. This was their birthright. It was the least we could pass on. At the time, even the *idea* of return felt unimaginable. We were up against a brutal regime, Russia – the second most powerful military on Earth – along with Iran, Hezbollah, and dozens of Iraqi militias. We were destined to lose. But still, I insisted: never compromise with the enemy. Resistance was our only path. In my videos on social media, I often said that even if only an inch of Syrian land remained free, I would stand on that inch. I wanted to inculcate these concepts: resistance, resilience, defiance. Surrendering wasn't an option, because I thought that that was what we needed in such difficult times. I pushed these messages for months, even as everything around us grew darker. I tried to be hopeful. When I watch those videos now, I'm astonished. I kept saying I was confident, that God wouldn't abandon us. I had no evidence – nothing concrete to back up those claims. But something made me say it anyway. I just wanted to instil hope. Why? I still don't know.

Instilling hope in those days was like asking someone to plant a tree in the desert. Imagine that. You're asking them to believe they're standing in a fertile orchard and that the tree will bear sweet fruit – when all around is dust and ruin. It drained me. I would go to bed utterly exhausted from speaking, from pretending I had energy left to give. But still, I insisted that God was with us.

The War in Ukraine

When the Russian invasion of Ukraine began dragging on, it gave us a strange kind of hope. I know how that sounds – selfish, even cynical, I guess. But it wasn't. We felt deeply for the Ukrainian people. They were strangers, but we understood their suffering. We knew what it meant to be targeted by a regime like Putin's. Their war meant Russia started pulling back some of its forces from Syria – especially air power – to redirect them to Ukraine. This gave us a sliver of hope. Perhaps their military focus was finally shifting. I even sent messages of solidarity to Ukrainians. Their resistance inspired us. Their enemy was ours. Russia had murdered our people and driven us from our homes. That regime – Putin and his cronies – will go down in history as war criminals.

The Russian partial withdrawal gave us a much-needed psychological boost. At last, I had something tangible to point to, something to support my belief that change might be possible, InshAllah.

At the same time, massive protests erupted in Iran, Assad's staunchest ally. This lifted our spirits too. I expressed solidarity with Iranian protestors and highlighted the atrocities Iran's regime committed in Syria. We knew change wouldn't come overnight, but militarily, things were beginning to shift.

I shot several frontline videos, sometimes just 200 to 300 meters from regime-controlled areas. I interviewed rebel fighters who reaffirmed their determination to keep fighting, no matter the odds. I shared these videos whenever morale was low, especially when the regime launched fake 'reconciliation' campaigns, urging civilians to return and surrender. I did the same when Assad regained international recognition, like his readmission into the Arab League or when certain countries normalised relations with him. Each time, I reminded people of our cause.

Even if foreign governments welcomed him, we would never accept him. A million people had died. Twelve million had fled. The country was destroyed. What did an embassy reopening change for us? We kept telling the world: this regime is a threat – not just to Syrians, but to everyone. It produces and traffics Captagon, trains extremists, and exports terrorism. Foreign governments turned a blind eye, caring only for their own interests. But it was still our duty to speak out.

The Death of Hassan Nasrallah

The windbag from Beirut's Dahiyeh. The news of his demise meant a lot to me. His death was not less significant for me than the fall of the Assad regime itself. In September 2024 Israel launched a series of attacks on Beirut, Lebanon. God forbid that I should glorify the Israeli military with my words, but along with millions of other Syrians I felt elated at the news of his demise, the demise of the leader of an organisation that had perpetrated massacres for years in Syria. Just to be clear. Israel this time didn't kill him because they were taking revenge for our children on our behalf. Israel and the United States let them come to Syria. Hezbollah entered Syria with Israel's silent approval.

I couldn't sleep that night, the night the criminal Hassan Nasrallah was murdered. Celebrations took place in many parts of Syria, and I was particularly emotional because I had a personal score to settle with him, with his whole organisation, the Lebanese Hezbollah, a terrorist organisation. The same terrorist organisation that occupied al-Qusayr and kicked me and my family out of our hometown. They killed my friends and members of my own family.

My cousin Salman lost his hand as a result of Hezbollah's attack on my uncle's house. The whole family was injured. They had already killed my uncle Abd al-Mawla Abu 'Ali, the same man who, in 2006, during the July war between Hezbollah and the Israelis, opened the door of his house to Lebanese refugees. As a reward for his hospitality, Hezbollah killed him and mutilated his children.

They killed my friend Tarad, the kindest person I've ever met. They killed him while he was filming the fighting. In the footage, you can hear Tarad utter his last words, namely the shahadah, there is no other God but Allah and Muhammad is God's prophet.

Then there is my other cousin, Khaled Abu Jihad. The first person to teach me how to read the Quran. To this day he's the person who deserves all the credit if I can read the holy book according to the rules of tajwid. He was also killed by Hezbollah.

I will never see again so many people I knew, so many people I loved. The criminal Hassan Nasrallah killed them. He and his terrorist organisation came to our country to fight us. He will answer to God for his crimes, for killing these wonderful people.

So, if you're still wondering why we consider Hezbollah a terrorist organisation, here is why. There are videos of Hezbollah members exulting and expressing their pride at the attack on my hometown. Their sectarian hatred resulted in hundreds of thousands of civilians killed. Other senior members of this self-defined Party of God, such as Wissam al-Tawil even filmed themselves aboard a helicopter dumping the infamous barrel bombs on residential areas in Syria. These barrel bombs landed on innocent civilians, killing them indiscriminately. That was not enough to satisfy these crooks; they even filmed themselves in the act. To all those who still consider it a resistance, who still think Hezbollah is fighting an existential war against Israel, let me tell you: they fought their existential war against us, against the Syrian Revolution. Let me refresh your memory a little. In 2011, when the Syrian Revolution broke out, Hezbollah declared its loyalty to the Assad regime against the Syrian population which had been demonstrating peacefully against authoritarianism. They immediately sent their military consultants to Damascus to instruct the regime on how to crack down on our protests. In 2012, their fighters entered Syria for the first time to fight secretly. They attacked our villages and killed civilians. Their leader, the criminal Hassan Nasrallah consistently denied their direct involvement with the events in Syria at this point. By 2013, they were present in large numbers in the Homs province. By now, they could no longer deny their presence in Syria. No one knows this more than me. I was there covering the events. They engaged in a brutal sectarian, genocidal offensive against us in Homs, my city. In 2014 and 2015, they launched another offensive, this time in the Qalamoun region, where they implemented the same scorched earth methodology, killing innocent civilians indiscriminately. People fled Qalamoun and its cities, among them Zabadani, which was hit particularly acutely, and they made their way to Madaya. Hezbollah then put a siege on Madaya, one of the fiercest, most brutal and wretched crimes against humanity in modern history. Nothing and nobody could enter this town, whose residents died of hunger. Hezbollah then launched a taunting media campaign with its own hashtag #in_solidarity_with_madaya – in the relevant videos they filmed themselves eating large meals, humiliating the people who had nothing to eat because of their siege. I don't remember any of the self-proclaimed intellectuals, who admire these crooks for their supposed anti-imperialist resistance, saying anything about this. They remained silent while our children died of hunger. I could go on for days about the crimes they have perpetrated in Aleppo, in Homs, in Daraa, in Deir Ezzor, anywhere and everywhere in Syria, really.

I think I've made my point and I hope people will understand why people around Syria celebrated Hezbollah's defeats.[11]

I was in Idlib the night Hassan Nasrallah was killed. The whole city was out on the streets celebrating, chanting slogans, honking, singing.

❖ ❖ ❖

Idlib, 28 September 2024

'*These people have the right to be celebrating, to be elated at the assassination of Hassan Nasrallah, the leader of Hezbollah, the criminal Lebanese organisation, the same organisation that kicked them out of their house and displaced them. These people have had their relatives and friends killed by the party of Hassan the thug. It's 2 a.m., thousands of people are still out on the street, expressing their joy. These same people have endured so much over the past fourteen years. The time has come for them to rejoice at the demise of the worst war criminal. They now await the demise of the one and biggest war criminal of all: Bashar al-Assad*.'[12]

A week or so after this, the bodies of Hassan Nasrallah and his designated successor Hashem Safieddine, as well as other of other high ups and members of the Iranian Pasdaran (Islamic Revolutionary Guard Corps, or IRGC) had not yet received burial. Hezbollah claimed that Israel wouldn't let them dig out their bodies. They were trying to get the United States and France involved, to be able to bury their own leader. I remember thinking. Where are their allies? Where is the Syrian air force? Where are the Russians and the Iranians? Only against Syrians they seemed to be able to show such efficiency and resolve. But even the Syrian regime let them down. Why wasn't Assad helping? All their allies treated them like toilet paper, they used them then they disposed of them. And yet, their units were still inside Syria, still stationed in different locations. Since they claimed to be fighting an existential war for the liberation of Palestine, I thought why are their forces not all fighting in Lebanon? Why are they in Syria?

Showdown

All those years, we knew we were preparing for the final battle. We would either win or perish. There was no middle ground. The countdown had begun. Wars and battles are never easy, especially the final one. In the past, losing a battle didn't feel like the end. There was always a second chance. After each loss, civilians would be evacuated, often to Idlib. But now, there was nowhere left to go. That fact weighed heavily on all of us. The pressure was enormous.

As for us reporters, there were four or five of us. We witnessed the build-up firsthand. We met with members of HTS (Hay'at Tahrir al-Sham), including Ahmed al-Sharaa and As'ad al-Shibani, as well as various military leaders. I attended these meetings with my new colleagues and close companions during those final weeks: Muhammad Daher, the cameraman; Ayham; Jamil Hassan; Muhammad Bel'as; Muhammad al-Faysal; and Sa'ad Zaydan. They were my brothers in this final chapter. The military leadership gathered us together when few knew the operation was coming. They told us plainly: the final battle was imminent. This wouldn't be just another operation, it would be decisive. Victory or annihilation. It was hard to respond. It's not easy to walk into a battle when you understand what's at stake. If we lost, it wouldn't just be another retreat. There would be no safe zone, no fallback. It would be the end.

Yet the leadership had reasons to believe this was the right time.

Intelligence indicated that the regime was preparing for a full-scale assault within the next year. Striking first would give us the upper hand. They were also confident in the extensive military training and logistical preparation they had carried out. The opposition had succeeded in manufacturing its own drones, stockpiling weapons, and recruiting thousands of dedicated fighters. Every element of the preparation, from strategy to execution, was rooted in Syrian hands and Syrian minds. At the decision-making level, all those involved were Syrian. No foreign state offered us arms, guidance, approval, or even basic support.

As'ad al-Shibani, now the Foreign Minister of the transitional government, even had meetings with foreign representatives to let them know a battle might begin at any time. He wanted to avoid diplomatic fallout, wanted no one to be 'surprised'. The reactions, even from supposedly 'friendly' governments, were largely indifferent. As long as we didn't disrupt their interests, they didn't care. All we asked was to be left alone. To fight for what was ours.

Preparations were underway across all sectors: diplomacy, military coordination, humanitarian readiness. We knew the risk, but we also knew what was at stake: our homes, our dignity, our future. From a military standpoint, the plan was simple in its goal: to retake our cities, neighbourhoods, and homes. But the obstacles were enormous. One of the most pressing concerns was the sheer number of regime forces arrayed against us. In meetings with military commanders, we discussed media strategies for every possible outcome: advancement, defeat, withdrawal, evacuation. We had to be ready to document it all.

I won't lie – we were terrified. We didn't know if we were going to survive. This was it. If we lost, we'd lose the last inch of land we held. Where would we go? How would we report on yet another defeat? It was the most difficult decision of all.

We were up against multiple enemies, but how many, exactly?

According to our military estimates, there were 22,800 regime fighters already stationed in areas bordering the northwest. To gauge the regime's readiness, we media activists spread word that a major offensive was coming. The goal was to provoke a reaction, to get a clearer view of their capabilities. The regime responded by reinforcing its troops with an additional 8,000 fighters, bringing the total to approximately 30,000. It was a staggering number, especially considering we were trying to break out from an isolated pocket. And yet, the Syrian Army itself wasn't our greatest concern. The real threat came from the Iranian, Iraqi, and Lebanese militias, and from the ever-present Russian air force, capable of striking us at any moment.

There were parts of the plan I wasn't privy to – and may never be. Some things will remain secret for years. But I'll share what I do know.

The regime's 30,000 fighters were arranged in three main groups – three concentric layers of defence.

The first layer, closest to us, was made up of regular Syrian soldiers, mostly conscripts. Many were ordinary Syrians forced into service through mandatory conscription. This showed how disposable they were to the regime. If war broke out, they'd be the first to die. The regime was willing to sacrifice them without hesitation.

The second layer was composed of high-ranking officers – elite units closely tied to Assad's inner circle.

The third layer was the most formidable: foreign fighters from Iran, Iraq, and Lebanon. These were the regime's heavy hitters. Even if we managed to break through the first two layers, this final ring could launch a deadly counteroffensive and erase everything we had gained.

So, the military leaders made a bold decision: attack the third layer first. But how? If it was the farthest from us, how could we strike it without first going through the others?

The plan was to deploy elite fighters – natives of the north and northwest – who knew the terrain intimately. Unlike the regime's forces, most of whom were foreign or from other parts of Syria, these fighters knew the secret backroads, dirt paths, and unmarked trails that crisscrossed the countryside. These fighters would bypass the first and second layers without engaging, infiltrating deep into enemy territory to strike the third layer, even from behind if possible.

This elite force was known as the Red Bands, named for the red head bands they wore. These were the units entrusted with the most dangerous operations. They had undergone extensive training and were equipped with specialised weapons. Their mission was to weaken or eliminate the third layer, then fight their way back as the larger offensive pushed forward.

When we first heard this plan, it sounded like a powerful card we could play.

But there were others.

In areas the regime couldn't fully occupy due to lack of manpower, it had planted landmines. For years, we had quietly trained specialists in mine clearance. These experts moved under cover of night or thick fog, equipped with tools to locate and disable the mines. In some cases, they left them in place, just defused, so the regime wouldn't notice anything had changed. This gave us tactical access to otherwise inaccessible areas. It was a secret operation, never publicly disclosed, but critical to our preparations. The battle was drawing near.

We had intelligence from the Hmeimim Air Base, Russia's main military installation in Syria. We knew they had enough ammunition and supplies for just one week of combat – unless Moscow sent rein-forcements. Even more crucially, we knew it took about 72 hours for a decision made in Moscow to be executed on the ground in Syria. Our goal was to retake as much territory as possible within those 72 hours – before the Russians could respond. If we succeeded, we could force a fait accompli and perhaps even discourage them from intervening at all.

The goal was ambitious: to reclaim the entire provinces of Aleppo, Idlib, and Hama. We estimated it would take a full year of fighting. I asked the military leaders if we had enough resources to sustain a year-long war. Especially given that no foreign country was supporting us.

I heard that Trump recently congratulated Erdoğan for 'taking over Syria', but no, sorry. This was a 100% Syrian decision. Türkiye gave us the green light, but nothing more. No promises, no backup, no supplies. The military commanders said yes, we had enough to last a year. But we had to reclaim at least two provinces: Idlib and Aleppo. Hama was the stretch goal.

As the day approached, so did the fear. Would I survive to see it? Would my colleagues? Would any of us die martyrs, reporting until our last breath? We met every day. I wasn't prepared to lose anyone. I feared for Muhammad, our cameraman, and for each member of the team. I thought to myself: even if we liberate all of Syria, what would it mean if these men didn't live to see it?

I am reminded of a poem:

> *And even if they return to you the old places,*
> *who will bring back your friends?*

But more than anything, I feared for my wife and children. I was their entire world. What would happen if I didn't come back? How would Bissan grow up without me? How would Adnan live not even knowing me? What about my wife? The burden of these thoughts was unbearable. To make matters worse, I learned that our town – on the northern outskirts of Idlib – was considered a key supply line. That meant it could be bombed at any moment.

I begged them: please, just let me know a few hours before the battle begins so I can move my family. I asked for three hours, enough time to drive my family to Salqin. After much pleading, they agreed. It was time to prepare.

I wrote my will and told my wife. If anything happened to me, she was to tell our children: *Forgive me.* Tell them I believed in this cause.

That I never sold out. That I fought until my last breath. Tell them about Khaled. Tell them that to reclaim Homs and Syria, sacrifices had to be made, and that, sadly, their father gave his life. I told her who to trust, and who not to. I had never brought this kind of talk home before. I'd always shielded them from the weight of my work. But this time was different. I had to tell her everything.

Operation Aggression Deterrence

I remember I was still awake that night. It must have been around 2 a.m. when I received the message. The operation was about to begin. A few hours later, at dawn, it would be X-hour. I immediately woke my wife. The time had come. She needed to pack and take the children to Salqin to stay with her sister. I told her what was going to happen. There was no more room for hiding the truth. I got dressed and drove them there, with Bissan sitting on my lap. Normally, she would sit in the back seat, but not this time – I wanted her as close as possible. I caressed her hair, combed it gently. Saying goodbye was unbearable. I hugged her tightly, wondering if this would be the last time I saw her.

I dropped them off and drove back to our house in Idlib. It was around 5 a.m. I prepared for the battle. Our media team set out, then quickly split into two groups to cover different axes. One group included Jamil, Muhammad Faysal, and Ayham. The other group – myself, Muhammad Daher, Muhammad Bel'as, and Abu 'Arab – headed toward Aleppo. That morning, we filmed the first videos announcing that the battle had begun. Then we moved toward the frontline positions where we expected clashes with the regime's militias to erupt.

By 5 a.m., members of the Red Bands had already begun infiltrating enemy lines. They had reached the third layer of regime fighters – the rear lines, composed of Iranian, Iraqi, and Lebanese forces. The offensive started there. We could hear the explosions in the distance, though nothing had yet reached our position.

Then it came.

The Red Bands attacked the regime's rear positions with heavy artillery, tanks, and drones, targeting communication towers as part of the offensive. This effectively severed communication between the regime's defensive layers and disrupted coordination among its military commanders.

As reporters, we had also entered the battle. We began covering the clashes in real time.

The regime responded by targeting our heavy artillery, while the Russian air force launched limited airstrikes. Their response wasn't particularly intense – they were acting without top-level orders, and we knew they only had enough supplies for a week of fighting. The regime suffered heavy losses. In the aftermath, we sent messages to surviving regime fighters, urging them to defect and join the opposition in the battle for liberation.

Aleppo

On the first day of fighting – 27 November 2024 – I released the first video officially declaring, at least to my followers, that the battle had begun.

'The military leadership of the Revolution has today launched a broad offensive against the regime and its allied militias from Iran, Lebanon, and Iraq. Right now, fighters from the Fath al-Mubin Battalion are initiating operations with the aim of liberating our country from foreign occupiers.

'The next few hours will be decisive, not only for the Syrian Revolution but for the future of Syria itself, of the whole Middle East. These men are your sons. They have risen to reclaim our land and are ready to give their lives for this battle of liberation.

'I speak now to civilians still under regime control and to the displaced who are scattered across the country: these fighters are coming to free you from the oppression of Assad and the Iranian militias. We've received hundreds of messages asking: "Where are the rebels?" Well, here they are – prepared to die for your freedom'.[13]

We were right in the middle of the clashes as they unfolded. We moved alongside the fighters as they advanced into Aleppo and its surrounding countryside. I still remember the name of the first village we liberated: Qubtan al-Jabal.

This village sat directly on the demarcation line between regime- and opposition-held territory. Normally, it was just a ten-minute drive from the nearest rebel-controlled village, Darat 'Ezzeh. But because of its sensitive location and the poor road conditions, winding, unstable routes over hills and mountains, we travelled by motorcycle, which was ideal for navigating the terrain.

When we entered Qubtan al-Jabal, the hills surrounding it were still under regime control. I realise how crazy that might sound – but we were too eager, too overwhelmed with emotion to wait. We wanted to announce the liberation immediately.

The entire operation was codenamed Rad' al-'Adwan, Arabic for 'Aggression Deterrence'. The goal was to push regime forces back from the southern part of Idlib and from Aleppo and its countryside. We hoped this would serve as a deterrent against the constant attacks on our densely populated strongholds in the northwest, *Little Syria*.

According to the military leadership, the operation was expected to take a full year. But the regime's rapid collapse, and that of its forces, led to developments we could never have imagined. God had other plans.

As we rode into Qubtan al-Jabal, a tank appeared in the distance, heading straight toward us. At first, we panicked. But the fighters reassured us: this was the first piece of spoils we had captured. The tank had been bombing us just hours earlier. Now, it was in our hands – ready to be turned against the regime.

From inside Qubtan al-Jabal, I filmed another video:

'Thank God Almighty – these tanks that once bombarded us now return to their rightful owners: the people.

'I'm standing here in the first village to be liberated as part of Operation Aggression Deterrence: Qubtan al-Jabal. Our morale is sky-high. Spirits are through the roof. We ask God to stand with us, to let us return to our cities and homes. Please, keep our fighters in your prayers.

'*Taking Qubtan al-Jabal was no easy task. The entire village was heavily defended with armoured vehicles and military barracks spread out across the surrounding hills. But Alhamdulillah, all these hills have now been taken. The whole village is free.*

'*We can still hear the sound of rockets – but for once, they're not being fired at civilians. They're being launched at the militias of the Assad regime.*

'*May God allow every refugee and every displaced person to return home. O Lord, be our helper. Protect our heroes. Strengthen our men*'.[14]

As we advanced, hill after hill, we lost our own, too. Blood was spilled on our side. As part of our media strategy, we made a conscious decision not to publicise our losses. We didn't want to lower the morale of our fighters or boost the confidence of the regime's supporters. So we focused entirely on showing our progress.

Many of our fighters advanced in armoured vehicles manufactured in Idlib, which we were proud of: the Karrar and Ra'd. I remember seeing blood dripping from those vehicles – the blood of martyrs. I saw their bodies. I saw the wounded.

This victory did not come easy. It came at a terrible cost.

We owe every inch of progress to the sacrifices of those men – especially in the early hours, when the fighting was most intense. Some of them had been standing beside us minutes earlier, laughing, talking, full of life. Then, in a moment, they were gone.

May God rest their souls. They gave everything for our freedom. The least we can do is remember them.

And yet, those sights didn't intimidate me. Quite the opposite, they galvanised me. I felt more determined than ever to do my part. These heroes didn't die in vain. Their children must not grow up as orphans without reason. If they could give their lives, how could I hesitate to give mine?

After taking Qubtan al-Jabal, we rode back toward Darat 'Ezzeh on our motorcycles. We thought the area had been secured, fully combed. But we were wrong.

Suddenly, bullets rained down on us, we'd been ambushed. For a terrifying few minutes, we had no cover, no support. Then, just in time, one of our pick-up trucks arrived, firing back with its mounted machine gun. By a miracle, we survived.

But that moment made one thing terrifyingly clear: we were going to be close to death, again and again. The nightmare of martyrdom wasn't over yet. But again – Alhamdulillah – we made it back safely to Darat 'Ezzeh. From there, we drove home, and I immediately got to work editing and uploading the first videos.

Fighting was underway across several areas of Aleppo Province. As members of the media team, we contacted the operations room for instructions on where to go. They informed us that our forces were making progress around Atareb and advancing toward Base 46.

I realise that name may not mean much to most people, but for us, Base 46 was monumental. It had been one of the largest military bases in Syria, since long before the Revolution. The regime had built massive military compounds near every major city to enforce its grip, and Base 46 was the key to Aleppo.

For years, rockets and drones were launched daily from that base, raining destruction on civilians. We came to associate every military operation that originated from Base 46 with horrific massacres. It became a symbol of regime brutality, so powerful, so entrenched, that I never imagined we could capture it, even if we liberated the entire country.

So when they told us it had fallen, I couldn't believe it. I had to see it with my own eyes.

I burst into tears. That base was our nightmare. How could it be over? Other villages were being liberated that night, but Base 46 was the moment. The next morning, I went there to film the first video from inside the base.

'Base 46, which for years terrified the people living around it, is now ours. It will no longer bring death. No more rockets. No more missiles.

'A few hours ago, the Military Operations Command confirmed the base's capture. One of the largest military bases in Syria has now been returned to its rightful owners: the people, Alhamdulillah.

'As part of the Aggression Deterrence operation, 140-square kilometres have been reclaimed so far. Since yesterday, 16 towns and villages around Base 46 have been liberated. The displaced residents of these areas can now return home. They can leave their tents behind.

'Our Lord has answered the prayers of the elderly, those in their sixties and seventies, who begged Him to let them live long enough to see this day, to see their homes again. We ask God to let them live long enough to witness the final victory, the fall of Bashar al-Assad, and the collapse of his criminal regime. Mothers who lost their sons, the mothers of our martyrs, can finally return to their homes.

'We've also captured 15 tanks from the base. These tanks will now serve the people of Syria, entrusted to the rebels who will use them justly, not to slaughter civilians, as the regime once did. Four armoured vehicles have also been seized. InshAllah, our fighters will make full use of these gains to liberate the rest of our land.

'The Aggression Deterrence operation continues. We've taken back more in one day than I ever dreamed possible. I never thought I would live to film this video from inside Base 46, but this is what God has willed. Towns are falling back into our hands one by one. Just a few hours ago, Urem al-Kubra became the latest to be liberated in Aleppo Province. We pray that all refugees and displaced families will soon return to their homes. People, keep our fighters in your prayers'.[15]

Once Base 46 fell, advancing toward the surrounding villages and towns became significantly easier. From where we stood, we could already see the skyline of Aleppo in the distance.

It didn't take long before the first civilians began returning to their homes. We warned them about the dangers: landmines, possible unexploded ordnance, and even small pockets of regime soldiers still hiding in the area. But they couldn't wait any longer. They needed to go home.

In Urem al-Sughra, we met an elderly woman who had been displaced for thirteen years. She had waited all that time to come back to her house. When we interviewed her, she was in tears – but her joy was undeniable. She had vowed to return, and now she was finally there.[16]

It was one of the most touching moments of the entire campaign. I was overwhelmed. I felt like my heart might burst from my chest.

After the rebels took Urem al-Kubra, Urem al-Sughra, Kafr Hamra, and Khan al-'Assal, the regime responded with a public announcement: they were preparing an imminent counteroffensive to retake the liberated areas.

But this was nothing more than a lie, a psychological tactic aimed at boosting the morale of its troops and supporters.

As members of the media team, it was our duty to debunk these false claims. My colleagues and I moved alongside the rebel fighters, documenting every step of the operation, until we reached the Damascus–Aleppo M5 motorway, Syria's main national artery, connecting the capital with its economic heart.

At that point, we were just a five-minute drive away from central Aleppo.

The regime continued pushing its propaganda machine, filled with lies, to boost the morale of its troops. It falsely claimed it had retaken the cities and areas seized by the rebels in the first few days of the offensive. Iranian and Russian media amplified these fabrications, spreading a narrative that regime forces were still in full control.

This made our job twice as hard.

Even some Syrians who supported the Revolution started to believe the regime's lies, like the claim that they had retaken Khan 'Assal in the Aleppo province. Our responsibility as media activists intensified. We had to expose the truth: the regime had not recaptured anything.

We worked under heavy artillery fire, rocket attacks, and airstrikes just to film the reality on the ground. All the while, the operation moved forward and on the evening of 29 November 2024, just around sunset, rebel forces entered Aleppo. The first clashes took place in its outskirts and residential areas. From behind the front lines, we followed the advance. As soon as our fighters took their first positions inside the city, I released a video on social media:

'The liberation of Aleppo has begun. The city stands on the verge of freedom. Regime forces, along with their Iranian allies, are collapsing on every front. Moments ago, we intercepted a radio transmission from an Assad army colonel calling for reinforcements. The response?

'"We have no more units – only generals."

'They've lost control. Since this morning, over 25 villages and towns have been liberated, some of them in highly strategic areas. The Military Operations Command has confirmed the capture of al-Hamadaniyyeh, al-Furqan, New Aleppo, and al-'Iss, a place forever etched in our memory for its fierce battles and for the regime's massive military presence there, especially among Iranian militias.

'Also liberated: al-Hadir, the regime's first line of defence on Aleppo's outskirts. Even Iranian media has confirmed their retreat.

'Meanwhile, in Idlib province, our forces have taken Khan al-Subul and Joubas. That means Saraqib and Ma'arrat al-Nu'man are next, it's only a matter of time. During the fighting, our men captured a T-90 tank.

'To our people in tents and refugee camps: liberation is under way.
Be hopeful, and keep our men in your prayers'.[17]

The liberation of al-Hadir and al-'Iss were especially symbolic.
These were strongholds, heavily fortified, once guarded by some of the
regime's most elite forces. Their fall marked the beginning of the end
for the regime in Aleppo.

From a media perspective, intercepting that radio call, hearing the
desperation, the loss of control, was a significant victory in the information war. It gave us undeniable proof of the regime's collapse.

But just as we were reporting the rebel advance into Aleppo, I
received devastating news: the Russian air force had targeted our neighbourhood, and an airstrike had hit the area near our home in Idlib. My
wife and children weren't home, but Daher, who had been filming my
videos, lived nearby with his family.

We quickly drove back there and found out that indeed a petrol
station close to our building had been hit. Thankfully, our homes were
still standing, but the psychological toll was enormous. We had to com-
partmentalise everything: maintain morale, expose regime lies, report
the battle, and, silently, carry the fear for our families' safety back home.
Hospitals in Idlib were also being bombed. But when I stood in front of
the camera, I had to appear strong, composed, and confident. I couldn't
show how terrified I was inside. I couldn't let my voice crack at the
thought of my children becoming the next target.

Since we had entered Aleppo late in the day, we faced another
dilemma. Some of us proposed waiting until morning to film inside the
city. Others, myself included, insisted we go now, despite the risks. And
so, we did.

We entered Syria's second-largest city, its former economic capital.
Aleppo was ours.

My first thought was: *When will we take back my city, Homs?* As I walked through Aleppo, I met activists from Idlib, Daraa, al-Ghoutah. I asked them all to promise: *We'll liberate Homs, too.* It felt like a dream back then, a utopian vision, but I truly believed it. I knew that we were on the right side of history.

I remember that night in Aleppo vividly: posters of Bashar al-Assad were ripped apart by ordinary citizens outside one of the notorious security branches where Syrians had been tortured to death. We shouted 'Hurriyyeh!' – freedom – in the heart of Aleppo. It was overwhelming.

We filmed the capture of security compounds and jails. One by one, the prisoners were freed. I interviewed an elderly man from Jisr al-Shughour who had spent eight years in prison without seeing his family. He cried as he spoke of the torture he endured in multiple dungeons before being sent to Aleppo's central prison. 'The regime is the terrorist', he told me. 'Not us. They are the ones who destroyed our country. Allahu Akbar. May God support you as we make Syria for Syrians, not for the Assad family'.

Between 30 November and 1 December 2024, rebel forces liberated village after village in Aleppo's eastern countryside, along with military base after military base. The advance led us to one of the regime's most infamous symbols: Aleppo's Military Academy.

This massive compound was where thousands of regime officers were trained, indoctrinated, really, to kill their own people. It was a factory of oppression, where hatred for ordinary Syrians was instilled from day one.

We drove around its dozens of buildings, passing tanks and stockpiles of weapons. And now, by God's will, the rebels had taken it. The regime had fled as '*God cast terror into their hearts*', as the Quran says, and the Academy became a thing of the past.

On 2 December, we captured Aleppo International Airport, a feat that had once felt unimaginable. For years, Iran had used that airport to smuggle in fighters and weapons. Now, we had cut off that supply line.

'*My fellow Syrians*', I said in a video filmed on the runway, '*look at this: the arrivals hall. When are you coming back to Syria? I hope this airport becomes fully functional again, for the Syrians exiled by this criminal regime to return home and see a liberated country. Let this airport become a source of joy and pride. This is the dream we're building*'.[18]

As our victories mounted and the world began to pay attention, we had to fend off slander. Accusations surfaced in the media calling us Zionists, claiming we were agents of Israel. The most ridiculous came from Al Jazeera's Jamal Rayyan, who dismissed our cause as part of a Zionist plot. Rayyan even tried to tie Hezbollah's recent defeats to our success, implying coordination with Israel. He had no idea that we had been preparing for this battle for years. This wasn't the first time he had incited hatred, not just against the Revolution, but also against Syrian refugees in Lebanon. But I ask: *We liberated our land from Iranian, Iraqi, and Lebanese militias, does that make us Zionists? Our martyrs died to free Syria. Their blood soaked this land.*

These claims were not only absurd, they were insulting.

In our darkest hour, we believed we were on the right side of history. And now, in our finest hour, we still believed it. Aleppo was ours. We could barely believe it. We were advancing. We were liberating Syria.

Next, our fighters headed toward the southern part of Idlib province, a region especially dear to me because I lived there for years. I'm talking about places such as Khan Shaykhoun, Saraqib, Ma'arrat al-Nu'man, Kafranbel, names I've mentioned countless times in this book. Places I missed with a deep ache. My heart felt like a knot.

And now, we were coming home.

Idlib

After liberating Aleppo and its military bases in their entirety, we set our sights on the southern part of Idlib province. Now that the north of the country was under our control and our rear was secure, we moved south.

Saraqib was the first city ahead of us. It had been occupied by the Assad regime, as well as by Hezbollah, Iran, and Russia. This city held immense military, strategic, political, and symbolic significance, located at the intersection of the M4 and M5 motorways, Syria's main transportation arteries. The M4 connects Latakia and Aleppo; the M5 connects Damascus and Aleppo, via Hama and Homs.

Assad and his Russian and Iranian allies had bent over backwards to hold on to Saraqib, which made it the site of some of the bloodiest battles over the years. I knew this city well. Back in 2019, we had attempted to recapture it, but we only managed to hold it for a few hours before the Russian air force and Hezbollah came and crushed us.

After so many years of bombing and fighting, half of Saraqib was in ruins. I could barely recognise its streets. The Military Operations Command discouraged civilians from entering due to the large number of landmines. It took longer than usual to declare it safe; engineers had to work carefully to clear it. But finally, we entered. It was the first liberated city in Idlib province, and I was thrilled.

On 30 November 2024, dozens of towns and villages were also

liberated in eastern Idlib province, Abu al-Duhur Air Base, Jarjanaz, Talmenes, just to name a few. Regime forces retreated quickly, and there were many reported cases of desertion, with fighters blaming one another. The Military Operations Command seized the regime's sudden collapse as an opportunity to liberate the entire province.

Saraqib had been heavily fortified and stocked with weapons. Once it fell, the regime's units behind it fled, causing a domino effect that allowed town after town to fall into rebel hands.

At this point, as I watched this unprecedented collapse unfold, city after city liberated, I found myself asking: *Was this really happening? Was this the moment we had waited for?*

After so many years of suffering, it felt unreal. Refugees in camps were going to return home. I had lost hope of ever seeing some of these places again. Particularly Ma'arrat al-Nu'man, where I had lived for years after we were kicked out of al-Qusayr. I had accepted that I'd never see it again. The same with Homs and al-Qusayr.

But as we approached Ma'arrat al-Nu'man, I felt that my heart would explode with emotion. I have already spoken about the mythical nature of this city, how it had been burned down and rebuilt seven times. Now, I was about to witness its eighth rebirth. When we finally entered Ma'arrat al-Nu'man, I was shouting with joy at the top of my lungs. This time, I chose to stay behind the camera, because the man who had been behind the camera for years, Muhammad Daher, is from Ma'arrat al-Nu'man himself. We had lived together. We had been expelled from that city together. He had always stood silently behind the lens, like an unknown soldier. This time, I wanted him to stand in front of it, returning to his hometown as a free man.

✦ ✦ ✦

I love Ma'arrat al-Nu'man and its people. They never allowed hardship to break them. They always found strength and resilience to start again. During the years I lived there, I never felt like a stranger. I never felt poor, even though I had nothing. Perhaps that's why they call it 'the city of the poor' – because you can live and thrive with very little. Its people are some of the most hospitable and kind-hearted anywhere. I had such a deep attachment to that city that I was as happy as when we entered Homs.

Next was Kafranbel, a place tied to very different but equally powerful emotions. I had also lived in Kafranbel. It's where I got married. It's where I built memories with my friends, the three heroes: Khaled, Ra'ed, and Hamoud. After everything I've said about Kafranbel in this book, you can probably imagine how I felt when the rebels liberated it. I was speechless. The joy I had felt in Ma'arrat al-Nu'man now turned into something spiritual in Kafranbel. I shivered. I felt Khaled, Ra'ed, and Hamoud watching over us. I wept. I could feel their presence beside me. Rationally, I knew they were gone – but something in me asked: *Could they be alive?*

For a brief moment, it felt like they had returned, and I had reunited with them again. I remembered Khaled's distinctive laugh, Hamoud's jokes, and Ra'ed's creativity and tireless work ethic. None of it had faded from my memory. I spent four of the most meaningful years of my life in that place, at Radio Fresh and with the Union of Revolutionary Bureaus. Those years were like a different world, filled with purpose and brotherhood. That place was my home. No words can truly capture what it meant to me.

By now, the building had been destroyed. But a climbing plant that Khaled and I once planted was still there, the only thing still standing amid the destruction. It had grown wildly, wrapping itself around every corner of our old office. No one had watered it. No one had tended to it. Yet it had survived and flourished. And I thought: *Exactly. That's our story.* They destroyed everything, but our plant still stands. Just like our Revolution, which has survived, and even flourished, despite everything.

Call me sentimental. Call it a metaphor. But that sight meant the world to me.

I had such beautiful memories in that place.

I ask God to grant mercy to the souls of Khaled, Ra'ed, and Hamoud.

How I wish they could have lived to see this day, to witness victory, to share in the joy.

After Kafranbel, dozens more towns and villages in southern Idlib were liberated: al-Habit, Haysh, Khan al-Subul, all the way down to Khan Shaykhoun, a large town that had long hosted regime military installations due to its strategic location: it's the last town before Idlib borders Hama province. To the regime, it was Hama's frontline defense. But when we entered Khan Shaykhoun on 1 December 2024, we saw destroyed regime tanks, and others still functional, abandoned by fleeing regime forces and quickly put to use by our fighters. The capture of Khan Shaykhoun meant that Idlib province was now fully under rebel control, and Hama was next.

Hama

As part of our media campaign, on 2 December 2024, we filmed videos at the entrance to the city, in front of the 'Welcome to Hama' sign, announcing the beginning of the battle inside Hama province. The fighting in Hama was brutal. The clashes there were some of the fiercest yet. Dozens of rebel fighters fell. The regime, having lost both Idlib and Aleppo, could not afford to lose a third province.

Between 2 and 3 December 2024, the rebels took Souran, on the M5 highway as well as Kafr Zita, Sayyad, Tall al-Sayyad, Tayyibat al-Imam, Halfaya, Ma'ardes, Qala't al-Madiq, Ltamneh, and Morek, among others. The rebels continued their remarkable advance, but at a high cost. Fighting remained intense, and the regime responded with hundreds of airstrikes, along with heavy artillery and rocket attacks, across multiple fronts around Hama. We were now a few miles away from Hama.

Among the fiercest clashes of the entire Hama campaign were those in Jabal Zayn al-'Abidin, a strategically critical mountain overlooking Hama and its countryside. This towering elevation had long served as a major artillery and surveillance post for the regime. They had stationed anti-tank guided missiles, tanks, and armoured vehicles on its slopes, making it a deadly stronghold. Capturing it was both symbolic and essential. The fighting was brutal, relentless shelling, close-quarter clashes, and heavy casualties on both sides.

We lost three entire assault groups made up of elite fighters during the initial attempts to take the mountain. They made progress but were then cut down by sniper fire and anti-tank weapons. Retrieving their bodies was extremely difficult. Because of the danger, the Military Operations Command barred us media personnel from entering the area until it was secure. Often, we couldn't even move, as fighter jets hovered overhead constantly. To this day, every time I drive past this mountain on the way to Homs or Hama, my heart aches. I think of all the young men who gave their lives there, for our freedom. Their blood stains those slopes. If it were up to me, I'd place a memorial on that mountain to remind Syrians of the price of liberation. Ultimately, the rebels captured Jabal Zayn al-'Abidin by surrounding and laying siege to it, which forced the regime's withdrawal. No battle was more painful or hard-fought than this one.

Because of the ongoing clashes, we had to take rural detours through backroads and small villages to reach Hama. As we approached Hama on the evening of 4 December 2024, as members of the media team and in coordination with the Military Operations Command, we released a video which served to counter the regime's propaganda about the ongoing events. Hama's province is populated by some of Syria's many minorities such as the Ismailis of Salamiyyeh. The regime lies claimed that our fighters were terrorists preparing to enter such cities to decapitate its people and wreak havoc. I spoke directly to the people:

'Large scale collapse of the regime and its allies in the Hama province. Widespread cases of desertion. They do not know where to go, they are running away like rats. The Military Operations Command is attacking the city of Hama from multiple fronts, and it is simultaneously securing its grip on its suburbs and countryside. They have captured large military installations and dozens of towns in the Hama province. People in Hama and its province, I turn to you, your date with freedom is approaching readily. It could be a matter of hours before freedom and your country return to you. I have a message for

you, a message from myself personally as one of you: I turn to the peo-
ple of Salamiyyeh specifically, I've always loved your city since before
the Revolution, and I know how strenuous you were in your support for
the Revolution. I know how much you suffered under siege and from
the regime's shabbihah. I turn to everyone in the province of Hama,
not just in Salamiyyeh. The men coming to you are your own children,
your sons, we are together in this. Did you see how things played out
in Aleppo? No one got touched, no civilians were harmed. Our men
brought safety to all areas of the city. I know that the shabbihah and
the so-called National Defense Forces are spreading rumours and lies
about what the rebels are coming there to do. The Military Operations
Command released a statement earlier assuming full responsibility for
everyone's safety. Our men are your children. Who can protect their
people better than them?

'I also have a message for the regime soldiers. I feel sorry for you
guys. Look around, where are your commanders? If they haven't fled
already, they're getting ready to. Same as they did in Aleppo and Idlib.
Hand yourselves in, as per the instructions that the Military Operations
Command has released: raise a white flag and drop whatever weapons
you have got on you. You still have time to make things right. Those
who have defected recently were able to get new IDs and are now going
back to their families. Don't let our men capture you, or worse, kill you.
This is our last call. This is the Military Operations Command's last
call. Don't turn yourself into cannon fodder while your commanders
are fleeing.

'The Military Operations Command released a statement earlier
for the people of Homs, for my people. I turn to you, your date with
freedom is approaching readily. InshAllah, same as Aleppo and Hama,
you will soon be free too. Be prepared and stay away from the regime's
men. Help our fighters when they get there'.[19]

Entering Hama, Umm al-Fida', or "mother of sacrifice", as we nick-named it, was also a very emotional moment. I've always felt a special bond with Hama. For me, as someone from Homs, Hama is our neigh-bour, and it was now free. We have a long-standing, amicable rivalry going on with Hama, but Hama is also the city where I taught for the first time, remember? Hama, with its iconic *norias*, (i.e. the ancient water wheels that turn gently along the banks of the Orontes River) is not just a city of beauty and tradition. It is also a city scarred by one of the darkest chapters in modern Syrian history. In 1982, it was razed to the ground by the Assad regime during a brutal military campaign led by Hafez al-Assad and his brother Rifaat, Bashar's father and uncle. Over the course of a few weeks, entire neighbourhoods were obliterated, and thousands of civilians were massacred, their voices silenced under the rubble. The memory of the Hama Massacre remains etched into the Syrian collective consciousness. For that reason, liberating Hama carried immense symbolic weight; this was not just about military victory, but about confronting a trauma embedded in the city's soul.

On 5 December 2025, Hama was sadiq, which means friend in Arabic but during those days it became a code word for 'liberated'. Again, a wonderful feeling. People were cheering on the streets, some of them recognised me as a I shot my videos for social media and greeted me or even joined me behind the camera, children with their slogans and women with their zaghroutas. Same as in Aleppo, we filmed the liberation of the city's central prison and people finally emerging from those dungeons. The city was resurrected at last.

If you watch the videos I posted on Instagram during the days lead-ing up to Hama's liberation, you'll notice that I always made it a point to remain professional and composed, focused on the task at hand. But the moment I saw the Orontes River, the same river that flows through my hometown of al-Qusayr, something inside me broke. The sight of Hama's iconic norias, gently turning beside the river, overwhelmed me.

I couldn't hold back the emotion.[20]

It wasn't just water or a landmark, it was a living thread connecting the past I was forced to leave behind with the present we were reclaiming. I stood there, stunned. For a moment, I simply couldn't believe it. Our dream had come true.

Shortly after the rebels entered the city, they advanced toward Hama's military airport, one of the most feared and notorious sites in Syria. For years, it had been a launching pad of death. Every time a plane took off from that base, we braced ourselves for news of yet another massacre. Until the final moments before its fall, it remained fully operational, contributing to the regime's campaign of terror against civilians. Its capture marked a turning point. It became the fifth military airport to fall into the hands of the rebels, and a major milestone in our liberation battle, not just strategically, but symbolically too. A fortress of death had been silenced, marking the complete liberation of Hama and its entire province.

Homs

We hadn't slept a single minute in over 48 hours. We were closely tracking every development on the ground, moving constantly between Hama, where the core of the fighting was taking place, and Idlib, where we returned to edit and upload our videos. Because the regime had cut off internet access in the areas it controlled, we had no choice but to travel back and forth between the two cities just to find a stable connection.

It was exhausting work physically and mentally demanding, and it required enormous stamina. At one point, we requested access to satellite internet to help us stay in the field and continue reporting without interruption, but those requests couldn't be fulfilled. So we made do, pushing ourselves beyond our limits, relying on sheer will to keep going up and down the roads, carrying footage and staying connected to the world.

Now that Hama, too, was sadiq, I thought we finally deserved a break, even just for one day. I wrapped up editing and uploaded all our videos, then drove home around 1 a.m., desperate for a few hours of sleep. But just as I lay down, I received a call from the Military Operations Command asking me to return immediately. At first, I resisted. I told them I was completely drained. I hadn't slept in two days. But eventually, I gave in.

When I arrived, I met with several commanders, particularly those originally from Homs. I could barely walk, shuffling around like a zombie, my body aching with fatigue. They told me that Hama was secure, and their sights were now set on Homs. That one word, Homs, woke me up completely. My exhaustion evaporated. I was wide awake again. At the time, there were rumours of a possible foreign-brokered deal, one that would halt the fighting and effectively partition Syria into two zones: Idlib, Hama, and Aleppo would remain under rebel control, while Homs and Latakia would be carved out into a separate statelet.

Hearing this was deeply upsetting, not just to me, but to everyone. We had come so close to the Capital of the Syrian Revolution, and now we were being told it might be lost to a political compromise? So when they told me that the next phase of the military operations was aimed at liberating Homs, it was a moment of profound relief. They asked us, as part of the media team, to start preparing the public narrative, to pave the way in people's minds and hearts for the return to my city.

I asked if it could wait until the next morning, but the answer was no. The fighters hadn't slept either. They were pushing through exhaustion to seize the momentum created by the regime's sudden collapse, and we had to match their determination. There was no time to rest.

We didn't waste another minute. The night between the 5th and 6th of December 2024, we set out immediately and began preparing the first videos announcing that Homs would be the next to be liberated. We filmed the video in the middle of the night, running on adrenaline and the sheer weight of the moment. As we wrapped up, news reached us: Damascus had risen. Rebel fighters had infiltrated the capital and were launching operations from within. The unthinkable was happening; the regime's stronghold was beginning to fracture. In the south, Qunaytrah, Daraa and Suwayda, which I hadn't been able to visit, were also now sadiq. One by one, the cities of Syria were reclaiming their freedom. We were doing it. We were witnessing the fall of the regime.

In my nighttime video, I once again addressed members of the Syrian army, urging them to defect and join the ranks of the rebels. Reports indicated that many regime commanders in the Homs province were already fleeing, mostly in three directions: Damascus, the Syrian coast, and Lebanon. This left their soldiers with very limited options. I reiterated what the Military Operations Command had already declared: they still had a chance to surrender peacefully, hand over their weapons, and return safely to their families. Just as we had done in Idlib, Aleppo, and Hama, Homs was now on the path to liberation. Entire military units were welcome to lay down their arms and hand themselves in. Nothing was going to stop our fighters, and I made clear how this was the last chance for those who wanted to surrender.

Another sleepless night, but it was absolutely worth it. We were determined to be there as the rebel forces entered Homs. We recorded several videos, building anticipation for that powerful moment when we would finally see Homs again. Watching those videos now, after all these months, I can barely hold back the tears. The emotions return just as strongly. I filmed one with a large military unit made up mostly of men from Idlib and its province, these guys recognised me and knew how much Homs meant to me. 'We are all *Hamasineh*', they kept shouting, meaning 'We are all from Homs'.

I also shot another video, this time with my fellow reporters. I jokingly called them traitors, since they had all witnessed the liberation of their hometowns except me. Of course, it was all in good fun, and they promised me we'd be in al-Qusayr soon. The video went viral on social media, and for days people stopped me in the street asking, 'Are your friends still traitors?' They got the joke.

As the military caravans prepared to advance southward towards Homs, Talbiseh and al-Rastan, two cities in the area between Hama, where we were coming from, and Homs, where were heading, rose against the regime even before the rebels reached them. Local rebel units had been stationed in these two cities, the largest in the northern part of the Homs province, but they had been in a long truce and under siege by the regime. As the events unfolded in the rest of the country, they were catalysed into picking up their weapons again and captured their cities from the regime's grip, but they were not able to capture the infrastructure connecting their towns to Homs, which is located approximately 20 or 30 km away. The Russian air force heavily bombed these two cities and targeted the motorway between Hama and Homs specifically, leading to the destruction of a bridge (which hasn't been repaired to this day). The Military Operations Command was urged to rescue Talbiseh and al-Rastan, to enter the Homs province. The sensible thing to do, so to say, would have been for us to wait for the rebels to advance and secure the area before we went in.

As for me and the rest of the media guys, though, we couldn't wait anymore. We were so eager to enter the Homs province, we decided to take matters into our own hands; we overtook the column of rebel military vehicles and drove towards the two cities without any military cover. We risked running into regime vehicles or being ambushed, but we didn't care. Luckily for us, the regime had deserted the area by then, so we didn't encounter any obstacles. When we got out of our car, the people welcomed us, thinking that we were fighters; when they realised it was us, they couldn't quite believe it – 'What are you guys doing here before them?' The rebel military convoy that we left behind caught up with us a few minutes later. Again, I lost my composure, I was daydreaming as we entered the Homs province, *al-Aradi al-Homsiyyeh*, Homsi land, even before the fighters arrived. We kept the promise we made to Abd al-Basit al-Sarout, to prostrate to God in gratitude the moment we entered the province. In the videos I posted on social media from inside al-Rastan, which is located right on the border between Homs and Hama, all I could say, as I shouted at the top of my lungs, was that I was grateful to God to have lived to see this.[21] I was crying. The incredible feeling of stepping on Homsi land after all those years of forced displacement, my God, cannot be described in words. For me it was like being resuscitated, like being awoken from a long coma, like putting my hands on a glass of water when I was dying of thirst, like receiving a cure for a terminal illness after losing purpose in life. God had decreed that we come back to our city. The way people welcomed us was also particularly touching. Random people the same age of my parents hugged me and my colleagues as if they were hugging their own children. They had been waiting for us, they had endured so much for so long.

After entering al-Rastan, since we had no internet access there, we had to drive back to Idlib again to be able to upload the videos. None of us had slept in days, but the stakes were too high. Our eyes were now set on the presidential palace in Damascus.

We filmed during the night again, as the rebels were approaching the outskirts of Damascus, al-Sham, the capital of Syria. That same night, we drove back south again for what was probably the best, most unforgettable moment for me: we were going to step into the city of Homs. On the way to central Homs, we encountered a group of young civilians walking along the road. Their clothes were torn, and they looked worn out, physically and emotionally. When we spoke to them, we learned they had just been released from al-Balouneh military prison, one of the most feared detention centres in Syria. It was known as the little Saydnaya of Homs. For years, horrifying stories had circulated about that place, executions without trial, bodies burned to erase the evidence. These young men confirmed many of those stories. They were battered, exhausted, and visibly shaken by what they had endured, but they were ecstatic to finally be free, to finally go home. Some were heading toward Hama, others to Idlib or Homs. It didn't matter how far they had to walk or what time it was. They just wanted to be with their families again.

Nobody wanted to sleep, because it would have been such a shame to miss those wonderful moments. As for me, there was no chance I would miss the moment we entered Homs. Not for anything in the world.

Setting foot in Homs's Clock Square was overwhelming. This wasn't just any public square. For me, and for so many others from Homs, it held immense symbolic significance. It was there, in that very spot, that I took part in my first ever protest. I remember it vividly, our voices rising in unison, full of hope and defiance, as we stood together against injustice. To return to that square now, after all the years of siege, destruction, displacement, and grief, felt like a full circle had been drawn. The place had changed, but the memories hadn't. Standing there was like standing in a living archive of our revolution. Every corner of that square held a memory – of chants, of banners, of friends no longer with us.

It wasn't just incredible. It was sacred. It was finally happening. I wasn't just returning to my city, I was keeping a promise. During those difficult days, so many people had reached out to me, asking, hoping, praying for the liberation of Homs. And I had promised them it would happen. I told them we would come back, that Homs would be free again.

But what did I really know at the time? I had no certainty. No guarantees. Only faith. Only hope. That promise came from the heart, not from any military strategy or insider knowledge. And yet, here we were. Back in Homs.

The promise, somehow, came true on 7 December 2024. It's impossible to fully describe the joy we felt that day. The same city from which the regime had expelled us, forcing us onto those green buses of humiliation. As some will probably remember, between 2015 and 2020 the Syrian regime used green buses as part of evacuation deals during the civil war. In Homs, for example, after besieging and recapturing opposition-held areas, these buses transported civilians and rebel fighters out of captured towns and cities to other opposition-controlled regions like Idlib. Of course, the regime presented these as humanitarian evacuations, but they were often forced displacements following intense military sieges, part of a strategy of demographic engineering and consolidating regime control over key areas such as Aleppo, Homs and Hama. We were now returning to our city, not as victims, but as liberators. We rode in on military vehicles, not as passengers of defeat, but as the bearers of hope.

We called ourselves the grandchildren of Khaled ibn al-Walid, and now we were back, entering the Khaled ibn al-Walid Mosque, a place of immense symbolic meaning for every person from Homs. That mosque had witnessed everything: our prayers, our protests, our pain, and now, our return. Now, we were about to pray *fajr* there again for the first time in years. As we stepped inside, the words rang out in our hearts:

'Ahfad Khaled ma biynamu 'ala dayyim' – [22] أحفاد خالد ماينامو على ضيم

The grandchildren of Khaled ibn al-Walid[23] do not remain silent under oppression.

❖ ❖ ❖

The atmosphere in Homs that night was electric, but also surreal. People poured into the streets, overwhelmed by emotion, some weeping, others shouting with joy, many simply stunned into silence. It was as if time had stopped and rewound itself. Faces I hadn't seen in over a decade appeared out of the crowds, older, more tired, but still familiar.

Some of the houses I passed still bore the scars of shelling, bullet holes marking the walls like open wounds. Entire neighbourhoods had been reduced to rubble, and yet people were returning, reclaiming what little remained. What struck me most was the resilience in their eyes, they had suffered so much, lost so much, but their spirit hadn't broken.

But Homs was no longer a memory or a dream. It was tangible again, filled with life and the noise of return. The people had come back, not just to mourn, but to rebuild, to reclaim what was rightfully theirs. I stood in the centre of the city as shots were being fired in the air in celebration, where chants for freedom once echoed, and I felt a strange mix of triumph and sorrow. We had returned as we said we would. Not just to visit, but to liberate. The promise had been fulfilled, but at such a cost. And yet, there was something holy in that moment. Something beyond grief or politics. Homs had waited for its children, and now they were home. No language can capture this feeling, neither Arabic nor English, nor any other human form of communication I think is capable of putting this wonderful feeling into words. Cameras cannot capture what our hearts felt – the pride.

At this point, it no longer made sense for us to keep driving back to Idlib to upload the videos. We began relying on local networks and patchy connections, which meant our coverage was slightly delayed. Still, we did what we could to stay online, to get the word out.

During the night between the 7th and 8th of December 2024, even with the poor internet, we began hearing the news we had long dreamed of: Bashar al-Assad had fled the country. Soon after, we received confirmation that all remaining military units in the capital had surrendered.

Game over.

On the morning of 8 December 2024, standing in Clock Square in Homs, I recorded the announcement I had been waiting a lifetime for:

'Congratulations, mabrouk, Syria. The crook has fallen. The regime has fallen. Long live Syria, and down with the Assad family. From Clock Square in Homs, I can finally say the words I've waited my whole life to say: the crook has fallen, Bashar al-Assad has fled the country, the Syrian Revolution has prevailed. Let the whole world know, we did it. Syria is celebrating. Syria is free at last, despite everything'.[24]

This was the best moment of my entire life. The moment victory was declared. Victory for the martyrs who gave their lives for our freedom.

Victory for the refugees who had spent years in tents, in freezing winters and burning summers.

Victory for the people who had been living among the rubble, who had lost their homes but never their dignity.

Victory for all Syrians who had stood firm and prevailed over some of the most brutal forces on Earth.

Much as I pride myself in possessing a good command of Arabic and being capable of articulating ideas clearly in my mother tongue, I couldn't find the words to talk about what we were living that morning of 8 December 2024. Everything was overwhelmingly stunning, breathtaking in its magnitude, indescribable, raw, triumphant, filled with a kind of beauty only born from struggle.

Damascus

Our next stop was Damascus. Or was it? Of course, as usual with me, I found myself facing yet another dilemma, torn between two choices. What about al-Qusayr my hometown, the place where everything began for me? Should I go there first? Or should I go down to the capital, Damascus? To al-Sham? We had to see it with our own eyes, to witness firsthand the unimaginable truth that the regime was truly gone. The traffic on the Homs-Damascus motorway was so intense it took us much longer than it normally would to get to Damascus. Rebel convoys were moving south toward the capital, while regime soldiers were retreating westward, toward the coastal regions – some of them even on foot. Later, the Military Operations Command issued a general amnesty, inviting these soldiers to return to Damascus, guaranteeing their safety until transitional courts could be set up to try those responsible for war crimes and to hold the criminals to account for their atrocities.

When we finally arrived in Umayyads Square, the most important square in all of Syria, I experienced something overwhelming in every sense, terrific in both the literal and emotional meanings of the word.

From the symbolic heart of Damascus, I made the announcement:[25]

The nightmare was over.

The regime had fallen.

And Syria was ours again.

And yet, as powerful as it was to stand in Umayyads Square, as surreal as it felt to say out loud that Damascus was free, my heart was already pulling me elsewhere.

Al-Qusayr.

The place where I was born. The city that shaped me. The ground that first taught me what it meant to love your country – and to lose it.

Al-Qusayr

As we left Damascus behind and turned towards al-Qusayr, I felt a different kind of anticipation. Damascus had been the capital of the Revolution's fall and rise. But al-Qusayr was personal. Every tree, every wall, every street there carried my own memories, my family's history, the voices of those we had lost.

The closer we got, the more overwhelming it became. I wasn't just going to witness a victory. I was going home.

The closer we got to al-Qusayr, the heavier my chest felt. I had dreamed of this moment for years, but now that it was actually happening, I was gripped by a new kind of fear – one I hadn't spoken about, not even to those closest to me.

What if, after everything we had achieved, I still couldn't go home?

Because unlike other cities that had been under regime control, al-Qusayr had become something else entirely – a full-fledged military base for Hezbollah. It haunted me: what if we had liberated the entire country, and yet my city remained closed off? What if I could return everywhere except home?

The thought was unbearable. I had lived through exile, displacement, siege, bombardment – but nothing, nothing compared to the idea that I might be denied the right to return to the very soil that made me who I am. So as we drove toward al-Qusayr, my heart was pounding – not just from excitement, but from dread. Would they let us in? Would we find snipers still stationed on the rooftops? Would we find mines where our orchards once were?

Alhamdulillah, on 10 December 2024, eleven years, six months, and four days later, I was home again. Despite everything, despite my fears, despite the years of occupation and destruction, I returned to al-Qusayr. Our Revolution prevailed, not just over Assad, but over Hezbollah too.[26]

The moment I entered al-Qusayr felt unreal. My eyes searched for familiar places, for signs of life, for pieces of the past I could still recognize. It had changed. Of course it had. War had scarred its walls and hollowed out its buildings. Some streets were unrecognisable. But the people were there. My people.

As soon as they saw us, they came running, old men, women, children, youth who had been just toddlers when we were expelled. I was enveloped in embraces. People I hadn't seen in more than a decade held me like a son, a brother, like someone who had returned from the dead. Their tears mixed with mine. Not one or two, everyone. Men and women, young and old. They didn't need to say anything. In that moment, tears said it all. Only crying can carry such depth of feeling. There are emotions that no words, no slogans, no celebrations can ever truly express – grief, relief, joy, vindication, disbelief, hope. Tears hold them all.

Crying is stronger than any other human form of expression. And on that day, in al-Qusayr, our tears weren't a sign of weakness. They were our final act of resistance, of survival, of reunion. Tears that washed away the dust of exile and bore witness to a truth that could no longer be denied: we were back, and this time, we were free. I looked into their faces, faces worn by years of suffering but still filled with defiance and dignity, and I felt something I hadn't felt in so long: wholeness. Like a circle that had been broken was finally being completed.

For the first time in so many years, I was no longer displaced.

I was home.

❖❖❖

After embracing my people, I went to see my family's home. It was destroyed, burned down, bare walls blackened by fire, everything else either looted or reduced to rubble. But I stood there, not in despair, but with a quiet, determined promise in my heart. I turned to what remained of our doorway, and I whispered to my parents,

'We will rebuild it. We will rebuild the whole town'.

This moment felt surreal, like the final scene in a film, the one where, after so much pain and struggle, the protagonist finally comes home. A happy ending.

We weren't used to those. Quite the opposite, in fact. But this time, it truly felt like one. A wonderful ending, carved out by our resilience, our sacrifice, our refusal to surrender.

I stepped into what used to be my bedroom, whatever was left of it, and it was like opening a door to the past. Memories flooded back. My childhood. My teenage years. My university days. The hours I spent there dreaming of something bigger, something freer.

I stood in the exact spot where I filmed my very first TV appearances as Samir Fathi. Remember? That small, makeshift set in my room, lit by a lamp and hope. I smiled through the dust and broken bricks.

I thought of all my friends from al-Qusayr, the ones we lost, the ones who gave their lives for us to be here. I thought of their voices, their laughter, their bravery. I thought of Tarad, of Khaled, of so many others whose names deserve to be etched into every wall we rebuild. Their absence filled the air, but so did their presence. Then I went for a walk around al-Qusayr. Just walked. Slowly. Every corner, every alley held a memory. I walked through the streets that raised me, past homes that once buzzed with life, past ruins that were once the centre of everything I knew.

And those moments, those quiet, aching, euphoric moments, will ever be the best of my entire life. I thought I could die this moment, and it would not matter. I could die happy.

8 December 2024

Epilogue

This is the end of the book, but it is not the end of the story.

We have a long road ahead of us, a road that winds through the wreckage of war and into the fragile dawn of what could become a better Syria. A Syria where our people finally feel safe. Where the law governs, not tyranny. Where no one is above justice, and no one is beneath dignity.

We still have so much to do.

We must build institutions, rebuild cities, and restore the trust that was shattered. We must give our children a country they'll be proud to call home – a Syria they don't have to flee from, a Syria they can carry with pride in their hearts.

And yes, we may still have more battles to fight. Against what remains of the Assad regime. Against attempts to drag the country back into chaos. Against the darkness that still lurks at the edges of our victory. But we are not afraid of the road ahead. Because we know who we are now. We've learned how to resist, how to rebuild, how to rise, again and again.

And rise we will.

Every time.

10 May 2025

Photographs — In Memoriam

At a protest. Hadi Abdullah, center, and Khaled al-'Issa on the right.

Above, clockwise: Hadi, Ra'ed al-Fares and Khaled al-'Issa; below: Hadi and Tarad al-Zuhouri.

Hadi with Hamoud Junayd.

Tarad al-Zuhouri and Hadi.

Tarad al-Zuhouri and Hadi.

Ra'ed al-Fares and Hadi.

Preparing a broadcast in Kafranbel at Radio Fresh, with Ra'ed al-Fares, center, and Ahmed Primo, right. Below: Hamoud Junayd, Ra'ed al-Fares and Hadi.

Hadi with Hamoud Junayd at the Union of Revolutionary Bureaus in Kafranbel.

Hamoud Junayd and Ra'ed al-Fares with Hadi at Hadi and Rafah's wedding in Kafranbel.

Hadi with Khaled al-'Issa.

Tarad al-Zuhouri and Hadi.

Hadi with cat and Tarad al-Zahouri.

Hamoud Junayd and Hadi with parakeet.

Ra'ed al-Fares and Hadi.

Khaled al-'Issa and Hadi.

Khaled al-'Issa and Hadi.

Left to right: Hadi, Khaled al-'Issa, Ra'ed al-Fares.

Hamoud Junayd and Hadi.

Tarad al-Zahouri and Hadi.

Khaled al-'Issa and Hadi.

Unknown fighter, Hadi, and Tarad al-Zahouri.

Foreground: Ra'ed al-Fares in neckbrace; standing behind,
left to right: Hamoud Junayd, Khaled al-'Issa, and Hadi.

Hadi with Ra'ed al-Fares and Khaled al-'Issa.

Hadi and Ra'ed al-Fares.

Ra'ed al-Fares and Hadi.

Hamoud Junayd and Ra'ed al-Fares, Radio Fresh Facebook page.

Radio Fresh and the URB (Union of Revolutionary Bureaus) after they were hit by regime aircraft, 7 December 2019. Screenshots from a video report on Hadi Abdullah's Facebook page. Details at the Syrian Archive: https://syrianarchive.org/en/investigations/ airstrikes-on-radio-fresh-and-the-union-of-revolutionary-bureaus

The destruction of Radio Fresh and the URB. Protest banners still hanging on the wall.

Hadi Abdullah reporting from the scene of the regime bombing Radio Fresh and the URB.
From the same video, more aircraft overhead at the site of the recent bombing.

Above: Khaled al-'Issa and Hadi.
Center: Khaled and Hadi, after being hit with schrapnel on the day before the assassination attempt.
Below: Hadi at Khaled's grave.

Top to bottom: Hadi's legs in July 2016 after the Aleppo assassination attempt; Hadi in his hospital bed, 6 July 2016; 'At the Gates of Aleppo': Hadi interviewing Hussam Abu Bakr, the nom de guerre of a commander in Haayat Tahrir al-Sham, filmed by Ra'ed al-Fares and posted to Hadi's YouTube channel, https://www.youtube.com/watch?v=2W7_WHr3G9U, 5 August 2016.

Top to bottom in Kafranbel: Banner in memoriam to journalist James Foley murdered by ISIS, Khaled al-'Issa on far left; Protest banner against Putin, with Khaled al-'Issa and Hadi standing behind the banner on right; Banner in an ironic tone, referencing U.S. President Barack Obama's 2007 campaign slogan 'Yes We Can', Khaled al-'Issa center-left. Unknown photographers, Facebook.

Top to bottom in Kafranbel: Ra'ed al-Fares with his poster showing Syria targeted as
the Dark Side of the Moon, referencing the Pink Floyd album; Banner in support of
the family of slain, unarmed Black American teenager Trayvon Martin, Khaled al-'Issa
in center and Hamoud Junayd, right; Banner in support of the Black Lives Matter
movement, Hadi standing behind the banner, right, and Khaled al-'Issa with arms
raised, back center-left. Unknown photographers, Facebook.

Notes

1 Gramsci, *Quaderno 3* [XX] § 34, trans. Quintin Hoare and Geoffrey Nowell Smith in *Selections from the Prison Notebooks*, International Publishers, 1971.

2 Hadi shows how he did this in an interview in 2025. See approximately minute 18:25. https://www.youtube.com/watch?v=xZON-5nFHdw&t=1112s

3 The Syrian Revolution General Commission, headquartered in Istanbul, combined dozens of anti-Assad Regime organisations into one opposition group with the mission of deposing him from power.

4 News broadcast, 12 April 2012, archived at https://m.youtube.com/watch?v=dHkR5umpuvE

5 'Syrian activist Hadi al-Abdallah fights to keep focus on the revolution', *al-Jazeera* archived on Hadi's YouTube channel 15 March 2015. https://www.youtube.com/watch?v=sZks5t8eMZk

6 The name Ra'ed means 'pioneer' in Arabic, in reference to Ra'ed Fares, Syrian journalist, activist and civil society leader from Kafranbel. He was the founder of Radio Fresh FM in 2013, an independent radio station reaching audiences in Idlib, Aleppo, and Hama provinces. Reporter Dana Ballout tells the story of Radio Fresh on *This American Life*, Episode 667, 'Act Two: Good Morning, Kafranbel', https://www.thisamericanlife.org/667/wartime-radio/act-two-11 ; also see Radio Fresh FM's YouTube channel: https://www.youtube.com/@freshfm90mhz/featured and Facebook page: https://www.facebook.com/radio.fresh.sy

7 Ra'ed's surname Fares means 'knight' in Arabic.

8 On 6 October 2015, the Free Syrian Army announced that it had destroyed 23 regime tanks. The event came to be remembered as 'majzarat al-dabbabat', literally the 'tanks massacre'.

9 A song whose title literally means 'Hello to death'.

10 https://www.youtube.com/watch?v=v8GiqoSRIGM

11 https://www.instagram.com/reel/DAG_3bmM8_b/ and also
   https://www.instagram.com/reel/DAdVDMIsgIK/

12 https://www.instagram.com/reel/DAcJBr8oeIX/

13 https://www.instagram.com/reel/DC4LUcrMia1/

14 https://www.instagram.com/reel/DC4TgXjsq8y/

15 https://www.instagram.Ra'ed.com/reel/DC6S8Yos5MB/ and

https://www.instagram.com/reel/DC7GUPEsY-6/

16 https://www.instagram.com/reel/DC9qKO1Mz8S/

17 https://www.instagram.com/reel/DC9TruwM5tY/

18 https://www.instagram.com/reel/DDFr09wMF6C/

19 https://www.instagram.com/reel/DDK3AsQsyq4/

20 https://www.instagram.com/reel/DDNh-n6MKmW/

21 https://www.instagram.com/reel/DDPAUJWsLQq/

22 https://www.instagram.com/reel/DDTmnImIpzs/

23 Khaled ibn al-Walid was the first Islamic leader to have brought Islam to Homs. The central mosque is named for him.

24 https://www.instagram.com/reel/DDTwCB9MbNM/

25 https://www.instagram.com/reel/DDUsnetMHxT

26 https://www.instagram.com/reel/DDZ54B9MIhg/

* All media is hotlinked in the ebook edition.

Banner to protest and raise awareness of the Assad regime using chemical weapons (CW) with Ra'ed al-Fares, center, holding flag. Archived on his Facebook page: https://www.facebook.com/raed.fares.5/ Unknown photographer.

Translator's Bibliography

Al-Haj Saleh, Yassin. *The Impossible Revolution: Making Sense of the Syrian Tragedy*. London: Hurst, 2017.

Creative Memory of The Syrian Revolution: https://creativememory.org/

Habib, S. (2017). Dying for a Cause Other Than God: Exploring the Non-religious Meanings of *Martyr* and *Shahīd*. *Australian Journal of Linguistics, 37*(3), 314–327. https://doi.org/10.1080/07268602.2017.1298395

Ismail, Salwa *the Rule of Violence – subjectivity, memory and government in Syria*, Cambridge University Press, 2018.

Malek, Alia. *The Home That Was Our Country: A Memoir of Syria*. United States, PublicAffairs, 2018.

Yassin-Kassab, Robin, and Al-Shami, Leila. *Burning Country: Syrians in Revolution and War*. London: Pluto Press, 2016.

Translator's Acknowledgments

This translation would not have been possible without the help of many people. First and foremost, my huge thanks to Carrie Paterson at DoppelHouse Press for agreeing to publish this book, showing great courage and a long-term outlook on Syria and humanity that no other publisher has demonstrated in my experience as a translator. Collaborating with her has been an extremely rewarding experience. Her unwavering support was instrumental in bringing this translation to life. Never change, Carrie.

Thanks also to Professor Michael Beard, whose comments, editorial guidance, and observations have been invaluable. His knowledge and sharp mind have aided this book into a far more thoughtful and compelling work than it could have been without him.

Thanks to my friend Haytham Alhamwi at Rethink Rebuild Society in Manchester for facilitating my first call with Hadi back in 2022 and for vouching for me with him. I'm also grateful to my former housemate in London *al-'Aghid* Khalil al-Haydar for helping me untangle some of the more intricate metaphors that appear throughout this book.

My gratitude also to journalist and author Asmaa Alghoul, whose memoir *A Rebel in Gaza* (Calmann-Lévy 2016; DoppelHouse 2018; Europa Editions 2024) offers another equally powerful account of life and resistance. Although we have never met in person, I first translated one of Asmaa's articles in 2011, and years later as I was working on Hadi's book, a fortuitous turn of events put us back in touch again, at which point she generously recommended I reach out to Carrie and DoppelHouse.

Finally, my heartfelt thanks to Hadi Abdullah himself for trusting me enough to let me translate and publish his memoirs in English, as well as for his tireless patience in clarifying the many passages that required further explanation.

www.ingramcontent.com/pod-product-compliance
Lightning Source LLC
Chambersburg PA
CBHW020439130626
46549CB00001B/207